# Rediscovering the Good News of the Gospel

# Rediscovering the Good News of the Gospel

*Asking the Right Questions
and Putting the Pieces Together*

BRUCE E. GIBSON

RESOURCE *Publications* • Eugene, Oregon

REDISCOVERING THE GOOD NEWS OF THE GOSPEL
Asking the Right Questions and Putting the Pieces Together

Copyright © 2025 Bruce E. Gibson. All rights reserved. Except for brief quotations in critical publications or reviews, no part of this book may be reproduced in any manner without prior written permission from the publisher. Write: Permissions, Wipf and Stock Publishers, 199 W. 8th Ave., Suite 3, Eugene, OR 97401.

Resource Publications
An Imprint of Wipf and Stock Publishers
199 W. 8th Ave., Suite 3
Eugene, OR 97401

www.wipfandstock.com

PAPERBACK ISBN: 979-8-3852-5660-0
HARDCOVER ISBN: 979-8-3852-5661-7
EBOOK ISBN: 979-8-3852-5662-4

09/18/25

Unless otherwise indicated, Scripture quotations are from the (NASB20) New American Standard Bible®, Copyright © 1960, 1971, 1977. 1995, 2020 by The Lockman Foundation. Used by permission. All rights reserved. www.lockman.org

Scripture quotations labeled NIV are from The Holy Bible, New INTERNATIONAL VERSION, NIV® Copyright © 1973, 1978, 1984, 2011 by Biblica, Inc. ® Used by permission. All rights reserved worldwide.

Unless otherwise indicated, Hebrew and Greek meanings or definitions are from Strong's Exhaustive Concordance of the Bible. Blue Letter Bible. https//www.blueletterbible.org

# Contents

| | | |
|---|---|---|
| *Preface* | | vii |
| Chapter 1 | Introduction | 1 |
| Chapter 2 | Impediments to Understanding the Full Message of the Gospel: Misunderstanding God's Heart | 9 |
| Chapter 3 | Impediments to Understanding the Full Message of the Gospel: Terminology | 32 |
| Chapter 4 | Impediments to Understanding the Full Message of the Gospel: Earning or Performing | 43 |
| Chapter 5 | What Has God Done for Us? | 49 |
| Chapter 6 | God Forgave All Our Sins | 52 |
| Chapter 7 | God Has a Plan for Your Deliverance, Freedom, and Salvation | 69 |
| Chapter 8 | God Placed Us In Christ | 74 |
| Chapter 9 | Who Was Included in Christ? Does All Mean All? | 84 |
| Chapter 10 | God Broke the Power of Sin and Death | 99 |
| Chapter 11 | God Caused Us to be Born Again | 111 |
| Chapter 12 | What is the Gospel? | 114 |
| *Appendix A: Passages from Acts that record what the apostles declared or preached.* | | 123 |

CONTENTS

*Appendix B: "ALL" Verses*     126

*Bibliography*     133

*Index of Scriptures Referenced in Chapter 6*     135

# Preface

I AM A VERY unlikely candidate to write a book—especially a book about the Good News of the Gospel. Writing a book was never part of my plans. Authorship never appeared on my bucket list. I do not consider myself a writer, except in the limited sense of my extensive experience drafting and revising legal contracts and purchase agreements for over 35 years. I do not appear qualified. In fact, some readers of this book will seek to discredit the conclusions I present simply because they do not believe I possess the proper credentials.

I freely acknowledge that I am not a theologian or an academic scholar. I have not studied Greek or Hebrew. I feel a bit like Moses, who questioned his own ability and qualifications when God called upon him. There are, of course, many scholarly books that address nearly all the topics I cover in this book—although none appear to consolidate them all—and many of these works are far more academic and detailed.

But the truth is that most of humanity are not theologians, and most do not think like theologians. The academic approach, while valuable, is often too intricate and technical for the average reader, who may choose to disregard a book authored by a scholar simply because it is difficult to digest. I do not think or process information the same way an academic might. And perhaps—just perhaps—God has enabled and entrusted me to write on this subject in a way that resonates with how a broader segment of humanity thinks, making it easier for them to grasp and process the Good News of the Gospel.

As you continue through this book, you will notice that my understanding of the Gospel has evolved over the span of 40 years. I never set out to depart from the mainstream views on evangelism or the Gospel. Rather, I have simply tried to follow the Lord's leading. There have been numerous moments throughout the years when Diane and I felt like outsiders. We held revelations in our hearts and posed questions that often left us feeling isolated. We rarely encountered voices that echoed our thoughts. Then, we would come across another encouraging book or message and realize we could never return to our former way of thinking.

Interestingly, as I prepare this final draft, we are in the process of replacing the carpet in three (3) bedrooms with hardwood floors. We began this project unaware of how disruptive it would be. At this moment, the piano, sofa, love seat, and recliner are sitting in the kitchen. The king-size master bed, dresser, chest, curio cabinet, and several other furniture pieces are crammed into the dining room. Dust covers everything. Just a few days ago, Diane and I commented that had we known how invasive this process would be, we might have opted for new carpet instead. However, in the past two days, as the floors are being stained, the chaos and inconvenience are suddenly starting to feel like a worthy investment.

In much the same way, the process of renovating my understanding of the Good News of the Gospel now seems profoundly worthwhile. If you are reading this book, I believe you have responded to God's invitation to discover more about His heart and His nature. I truly believe this book could be one of the many tools God uses to reach you.

One thing I know for certain is that God is both willing and able to expose false beliefs—whether about Himself, yourself, or humanity—and replace them with His truth. But that process begins with acknowledging those false beliefs, and eventually, exchanging them for truth. It can be exhausting and isolating, yet more and more people today are embarking on this journey of seeking truth, asking the difficult questions about doctrines and traditions, and choosing to trade in long-held misconceptions for liberating truth. Resources are more abundant than ever. There are pioneers who have courageously blazed the trail for you and me—and for them, we are deeply grateful.

I have often likened the process of replacing false beliefs with truth to that of a home renovation. Renovations are messy, they demand deconstruction, and they disrupt our familiar routines. Within this context, I frequently reflect on Jeremiah 1:9–10 as a blueprint for how God works in us and in our communities: "Then the LORD stretched out His hand and touched my mouth, and the LORD said to me, 'Behold, I have put My words in your mouth. See, I have appointed you this day over the nations and over the kingdoms, to root out and to tear down, to destroy and to overthrow, to build and to plant.'"

Notice the four (4) deconstructive verbs: root out, tear down, destroy, and overthrow, in contrast with only two (2) constructive verbs: build and plant. This clearly suggests that we often have far more to unlearn than we have to learn, largely due to how we've been taught and what we've come to believe. And as many of us know, unlearning is significantly more challenging and painful than learning.

But just like our hardwood floors, the work of renovation—of your understanding and perspective of God's heart for humanity—will be worth your investment. God is inviting you to see more clearly His beautiful heart and His divine plan for mankind—the Good News of the Gospel. However, that might require you to first unlearn, reject, root out, tear down, destroy, and overthrow some deeply cherished beliefs you've long assumed to be true.

Certainly, history and tradition alone do not guarantee that a belief is correct. Neither do zeal and passion—which Paul confirms when he writes that the Jews "have a zeal for God, but not in accordance with knowledge" (Romans 10:2). Your history, tradition, zeal, and passion may have served you well in many ways—but only God knows where they might have hindered your full understanding of the Good News of the Gospel.

# Chapter 1

## Introduction

IN ACTS CHAPTERS 4 and 5, we witness the Lord working powerfully through the apostles, using them as instruments of miraculous transformation. The sick were healed, and those tormented by unclean spirits were delivered. It must have been a profoundly awe-inspiring time, with clear, unmistakable evidence that the Kingdom of God had come in power. Yet, the apostles were not sent merely to perform miracles; their primary mission was to proclaim the Good News. Still, these supernatural acts did not go unnoticed—they attracted the attention of the high priest and the religious leaders.

Acts 5:17–18 records their reaction: "But the high priest stood up, along with all his associates (that is the sect of the Sadducees), and they were filled with jealousy. $^{18}$They laid hands on the apostles and put them in a public prison." It's worth asking—why would anyone oppose healing the sick or freeing the oppressed? What kind of heart resists such acts of mercy? The religious leaders didn't necessarily oppose the miracles themselves. What they opposed was the message that accompanied those miracles. Acts 5:28 clarifies their grievance: "saying, We gave you strict orders not to continue teaching in this name." The true point of contention was not the deeds, but the name—the Gospel message the apostles declared. Their message was so threatening to the religious establishment that it led to their imprisonment.

"But the angel of the Lord by night opened the prison doors, and brought them forth, and said, Go, stand and speak in the temple to the people all the words of this life" (Acts 5:19-20). That phrase—"this life"—suggests something radically different, a way of living and believing that was unlike anything the people had previously known or experienced.

What fascinates me is the specificity of the angel's command. The apostles were to return to the very place of their arrest. And their charge was to declare "all the words of this life." The NASB95 translation renders this: "the whole message of this life." That's not just a phrase—it's a calling. And I believe it remains just as relevant today.

Years ago, when I first read this passage, it stirred a deep question in my spirit: Was I proclaiming the whole message of this life, or merely a fragment of it? I began to realize that the Gospel—while true—can be presented in a way that is partial and incomplete. And while many followers of Jesus recognize that something is missing from what we commonly call "the Gospel," it is far more difficult to identify what's missing and integrate it into the full picture.

Have you ever believed you'd found the missing piece of the Gospel puzzle, only to later realize your focus had been off-center? In the 1980s, I was part of the charismatic—or "gifts"—movement that had gained traction in the 1970s. This movement sought to restore the gifts of the Spirit to the church and recognize the continuing role of apostles and prophets. These pursuits were—and still are—scripturally grounded. But after three decades within the movement, I came to a sobering conclusion: while these emphases are important, they do not, by themselves, complete the Gospel message.

To be clear, I fully affirm the operation of spiritual gifts and the vital roles of apostles and prophets within the body of Christ.

## INTRODUCTION

But if these are built upon an incomplete Gospel, we still lack the necessary foundation. Despite all the restoration, there remains a struggle within the church to clearly and fully proclaim "all the words of this life."

For others, the missing piece may have appeared to be the social Gospel—the call to care for the poor, the marginalized, and the oppressed. This, too, is a vital expression of the Gospel. Jesus deeply cared for every person, regardless of their status: the impoverished and the privileged, the sick and the healthy, the oppressed and their oppressors. Yet His ultimate focus was not humanitarian reform—it was the announcement and embodiment of the Kingdom of God.

Rooted in Enlightenment ideals, the social Gospel sought to build a better society through moral progress. And it has indeed accomplished meaningful good. But like the charismatic movement, if it is superimposed on an incomplete Gospel, it too falls short of offering the full message of this new life.

The same is true for many well-intentioned movements or emphases: evangelism, missions, spiritual warfare, social justice, homeschooling, the Daniel fast, 24/7 prayer, identity teachings, and more. All of these have value, but their effectiveness is limited if they rest on a fragmented understanding of the Gospel. The foundation must be sound for the house to stand.

In 2023, I felt compelled to seek a deeper revelation. I began praying more earnestly that the Lord—our gracious Father—would reveal the complete message of the Gospel. As part of a course I teach at a Christian university, I assign students to write their personal definition of the Gospel. To my dismay, nearly every response centered around sin, wrath, judgment, and separation. That recurring theme only reinforced the urgency I felt: we are not yet declaring the full message of the Good News.

I began asking myself a difficult question: Is the message I've shared over the years truly Good News? Or is it simply a message that reinforces division—separating the righteous from the unrighteous, the insiders from the outsiders? If we're honest, much of what has been labeled "the Gospel" doesn't sound like Good News at all. I should have seen it sooner: if your message only sounds like Good News to your group—and not to the rest of humanity—it's likely incomplete at best, and possibly even misaligned with the heart of God.

So why write this book? My purpose is not to discard what I've learned in the past, but to share, as clearly and humbly as I can, the broader vision of the Good News—the full message of this life—as I've received it through the Spirit of Truth. I don't claim to have arrived at perfect understanding. I haven't before, and I surely haven't now. But I do believe the picture is becoming clearer. Yes, there are still questions—gaps in the puzzle—and I acknowledge some of them throughout this book. The journey continues, but I now see a more cohesive, love-centered vision that better reflects the character of our God whose very nature is totally, completely, and always Love.

Proclaiming the Gospel is a sacred trust. As Paul reminds us in 1 Thessalonians 2:4, we are entrusted with the message. In today's terms, we might say we bear a fiduciary responsibility—to faithfully and selflessly represent the truth we've been given. What I offer here is not a final word, but an invitation. I don't expect you to adopt my understanding wholesale. But I do hope to provoke thoughtful questions, offer Spirit-led insights, and encourage you to seek truth—not just with your mind, but with your heart.

Ask the Spirit of Truth to lead you, to uncover a deeper and more complete understanding of the Good News. Because Good News is magnetic—it draws people in. If the Gospel we present is regularly rejected by unbelievers, then maybe—just maybe—it isn't the whole message. Understanding begins with God's heart. And sometimes, to see God's heart clearly, the Spirit must first dismantle false images, correcting distortions of God's nature we've long accepted. That, too, is part of the process. But it's a process worth embracing—for it leads us deeper into the life He always intended for us.

We can make the Bible say what we think it's supposed to say. We can even make the Bible say what we want it to say. While God's Word is true and inerrant, our interpretations and applications of that Word are not necessarily so. As one wise person observed, "a belief in an inspired Bible is not the same as believing all interpretations of it are inerrant."[1] Every cult or fringe movement has based its teachings on Scripture. Even the Pharisees and religious leaders, though immersed in the Scriptures, still missed the Messiah. "You examine the Scriptures because you think that in them you have eternal life; and it is those very Scriptures that testify about Me; and yet you are unwilling to come to Me so that you may have life" (John 5:39–40).

Let me share a true story—unlikely to happen again—but one that illustrates the point clearly. In August 1987, a year out of law school, Diane and I were married. By September, we found ourselves helping to plant a new church. We quickly got involved, volunteering in different capacities. Although I hadn't been publicly recognized for it yet, I sensed a call and gifting to teach. I volunteered to lead the young adults' Sunday school class. It went well, and before long I was invited to teach in the main service.

In 1988, recognizing my desire to grow as a Bible teacher, Diane gave me several study resources for Christmas, including a 7-pound Strong's Concordance and Vine's Expository Dictionary. I dove in with great enthusiasm. Later that year, as Christmas approached in 1989, I prepared a three-week teaching series on the three gifts brought by the Wise Men—gold, frankincense, and myrrh—and their symbolic meanings. I was excited to use Strong's Concordance. I looked up the meanings for gold (G5557), frankincense (G3030), and myrrh (G4666)—or so I thought.

What I didn't realize at the time was that Strong's numbers differentiate between Hebrew (H) and Greek (G) words. Mistakenly, I used Hebrew definitions for what were supposed to be Greek terms. The Hebrew word H5557 (instead of G5557) means "to twist, pervert, distort, overturn, ruin"—a stark contrast to the Greek meaning, "precious things made of gold, golden ornaments." Surprised but undeterred, I went ahead and built a lesson around this mistaken definition of "gold." I can't recall how I tied that definition into the nativity story, but somehow, I did. I moved on

1. MacDonald, The Evangelical Universalist, 9.

to week two. For frankincense, I used H3030, which means "memorial of God"—again, not entirely off base, but still incorrect in context. Week three followed the same flawed approach with myrrh using H4666, meaning "spreading out, thing spread out." The point is simple and sobering: I unknowingly made the Scriptures fit what I wanted to say. I shaped the message around what I thought the Bible meant. Then I congratulated myself for being "biblical." In hindsight, it was the kind of thing a Pharisee might do.

## TWO TREES IN THE GARDEN

Between 2001 and 2012, Diane and I hosted and pastored a home church we called Hungry Hearts. Some nights we had up to 40 people gathered in our living room, with fellowship often extending late into the night. Those years were spiritually rich and deeply formative—for us and for many who attended. While working full time in corporate America and raising four homeschooled children, I carried the responsibility of teaching most weeks. The teaching was not conventional preaching—it was interactive, conversational, and, as a result, much deeper and more dynamic.

One evening, just as we were about to begin, I sensed the Lord speak to my heart: *"Jesus was the Tree of Life in the garden."* It came as both a shock and a profound insight. I had prepared another message, but the impression was so strong, I set aside my notes and taught on this concept after only a few minutes of reflection. Later, I dove into Scripture to explore this more fully. That night marked a turning point in my understanding. I began to see that much of the church's message has been centered on removing sin—restoring humanity to its pre-fall condition.

But being sinless was not the end goal for Adam and Eve— and it's not the end goal for us either.[2] Adam and Eve were created without sin, but they were still incomplete. I'll say that again: being

---

2. If you struggle with Jesus being the Tree of Life consider what Paul said in 1 Corinthians 10:4 regarding Jesus being the rock from which Israel drank in the wilderness: "and all drank the same spiritual drink, for they were drinking from a spiritual rock which followed them; and the rock was Christ."

sinless—or forgiven—is not the same as being complete or mature. Even in their original innocence, Adam and Eve stood before an invitation to become complete by partaking of the Tree of Life—who is Christ.

This obscure but powerful thought became one of the roots of this book. I followed that insight then, and it's continued to grow ever since. That night, I saw a set of equations in my mind that expressed the revelation:

> Man + Sin ≠ Completeness (Christlikeness)
> Even if you subtract sin, man still is not complete.
> Man—Sin ≠ Completeness (Christlikeness)
> You must partake of Christ—the Tree of Life.
> Man—Sin + Christ = Completeness (Christlikeness)

To me, these equations underscored a crucial truth: removing sin or receiving forgiveness is not the end goal—it's the starting point. If the Gospel message centers only on forgiveness, it is not only incomplete, it is impoverished. Forgiveness is essential, but if it obscures or delays the deeper message of transformation and divine union, it limits what God is truly inviting us into.

God didn't place two trees in the garden to trap humanity. He placed them to offer a choice: a divine opportunity to choose eternal life. For years, I believed that if Adam and Eve had just avoided the tree of knowledge of good and evil, all would have been well. But I've come to believe that refraining from sin alone was never God's full plan. His true desire was that humanity would eat from the Tree of Life—Christ Himself—and receive the divine nature. Revelation 2:7 affirms this invitation: "The one who has an ear, let him hear what the Spirit says to the churches. To the one who overcomes, I will grant to eat from the tree of life, which is in the Paradise of God." Jesus is that Tree.

Why, then, were Adam and Eve tempted "to become like God"? Because they were already created in His image and carried within them the God-given desire to reflect His glory. That desire wasn't misplaced—it was divinely implanted. The only question was how they would seek to fulfill it: through self-effort and knowledge, or through divine life in Christ? By choosing the tree of knowledge of good and evil, they tried to become something they already were, but apart from relationship with and trust in God.

Genesis 1:26–27: "Then God said, 'Let Us make mankind in Our image, according to Our likeness. . .' So God created man in His own image, in the image of God He created him; male and female He created them." Humanity was created with the capacity to be like God. And though created without sin, Adam and Eve were not yet complete. God gave them a choice—a path to maturity. They could attempt to reach godlikeness through self-reliance (the tree of knowledge of good and evil), or through relationship and intimacy (the Tree of Life, Christ). Had they eaten first from the Tree of Life, the lure of the other tree would have lost its power.

God's destiny for humanity was not merely sinlessness. It was divine fullness—to rule, reign, and reflect His glory through participation in His life. Simply having your sins forgiven returns you to the condition of Adam and Eve before the fall. But even in that condition, they still had a choice to become complete.

And so do you!

You have an invitation that goes far beyond forgiveness: to embody and express the glory of God, to partake of His life, and to live from the fullness of Christ. The Gospel is not just about being cleansed from sin. It is about being filled with Christ. Are you willing to explore these deeper questions? Are you ready to let the Spirit challenge long-held beliefs, or would you prefer those beliefs go unchallenged?

# Chapter 2

## Impediments to Understanding the Full Message of the Gospel
*Misunderstanding God's Heart*

While each of us likely does not have a comprehensive and complete understanding of the Gospel or God's heart, no believer or evangelical or follower of Christ purposely sets out to believe less than the whole message of the new life. We do not choose to receive and believe less than the whole message. But we do not know what we do not know. Therefore, how do you even begin to question the beliefs and the approach that you believed for decades, and that your parents and grandparents believed before you? It, of course, is God's grace that plants a question in our minds or pricks our hearts, or causes an internal conflict that we cannot either ignore or resolve. Unfortunately, we have not been encouraged to ask questions or question doctrine; therefore, it has been easy to suppress the leading of the Spirit of Truth.

Specifically for me, I recall a couple of instances where God challenged my thinking by asking me a question. Several years ago, the Lord asked me this simple question, "If Jesus was the Son of God, why did He call Himself the Son of Man?" Thinking about and studying this simple question for hours and making notes, which I ultimately shared, opened up a whole aspect that I had never seen of Jesus's role as the Last Adam and the Second Man. On another occasion, I recall the Lord told me that I would no longer be able to ignore the apparent inconsistency of a verse and my belief system. I had to face the fact that not everything *appears* congruent. I had to acknowledge and make room for uncertainty. Scripture calls this a mystery. But mysteries ultimately are intended to be revealed, and God is faithfully revealing the mysteries to this day. Colossians 1:26–27 "that is, the mystery which had been hidden from the past ages and generations, *but now has been revealed to His saints,* ²⁷to whom God willed to make known what the wealth of the glory of this mystery among the Gentiles is, the mystery that is Christ in you, the hope of glory."

Because no believers or followers of Christ set out to believe less than the whole message of the new life, we are usually unaware of our own incomplete Gospel, and we can become very defensive when our belief systems get challenged. However, we often live with a false or incomplete view of ourselves, our value, and God's Love for us. We live with a false or incomplete view of God and His amazing, unearned, unconditional, never-ending Love for us that will never be reduced or withdrawn. We live with a false belief that because we feel unlovable, God could not love us. Therefore, if our foundation of belief about ourselves or God is wrong or incomplete, simply reading the Bible more, participating in another book study or men's group, or engaging in other spiritual disciplines, will not be sufficient to destroy the misperception or lie and replace it with the truth unless there is a divine revelation of truth. In fact, you will read the Bible and build a case from it to support your erroneous view of God or your erroneous view of yourself. All we need to do is look back in time at people and denominations that held on to a tradition or error while using the Scripture to build their case to hold on to error. While it is true that Scripture is our guide and the filter for hearing God's voice, it is also true that we often interpret Scripture without the inspiration of the Holy Spirit. In other words, we all hold on to and believe a wrong view of God, ourselves, and the Gospel. If we are interpreting Scripture incorrectly, and the Holy Spirit speaks truth about God, ourselves, the Gospel, etc., it will by necessity contradict the wrong or incomplete interpretation of the Scripture we have held, and we may accuse the "Spirit of Truth" of heresy. The Spirit of Truth enables us to abandon our false, wrong, or incomplete interpretation of Scripture in order to receive His revelation. Lord, we need Your grace to recognize the lies we believe about You and the lies that we believe about ourselves. I welcome you to expose the lies and replace them with truth. I hope you welcome the Spirit of Truth to expose lies and replace them with truth as well.

Paul refers to this revelation work of the Spirit in Ephesians 1:17–18: "that the God of our Lord Jesus Christ, the Father of glory, may give you a spirit of wisdom and of revelation in the knowledge of Him. $^{18}$I pray that the eyes of your heart may be enlightened, so that you will know what is the hope of His calling, what are the riches of the glory of His inheritance in the saints." The only way we function in wisdom and revelation is for the Spirit to sovereignly open our eyes and hearts. (See also Colossians 1:9 "For this reason we also, since the day we heard about it, have not ceased praying for you and asking that you may be filled with the knowledge of His will in all spiritual wisdom and understanding.") I believe the Spirit is still doing that work. I believe that the Spirit is still doing that work in you because He is so faithful.

And Jesus set the stage for this revelation work in Luke 4:18:

> "THE SPIRIT OF THE LORD IS UPON ME,
> BECAUSE HE ANOINTED ME TO BRING GOOD NEWS TO THE POOR.
> HE HAS SENT ME TO PROCLAIM RELEASE TO CAPTIVES,
> AND RECOVERY OF SIGHT TO THE BLIND,
> TO SET FREE THOSE WHO ARE OPPRESSED."

Jesus brought and is bringing Good News (the Gospel), but being blind hinders our seeing and receiving the Good News; therefore, Jesus not only brings the Good News, but He also heals the sight of those who are blind so that they may see and receive the Good News. And He is still doing that work. He is inviting us to let Him do that work in each of our hearts. The very familiar verse from Isaiah 9:2 is another analogy speaking of His power and work to enable us to see what we previously could not see, "The people who walk in darkness will see a great light; Those who live in a dark land, the light will shine on them." Moving from darkness to light is the Kingdom of God (Colossians 1:13 "For He rescued us from the domain of darkness, and transferred us to the kingdom of His beloved Son."). In fact, the opposite of the domain of darkness is the Kingdom of God.

"Jesus said, 'For judgment I came into this world, so that those who do not see may see, and those who see may become blind'" (John 9:39). In Christ's goodness, if you think you have a full picture of the Gospel, His first act of grace in the matter is to reveal to you that you do not have the full message of this new life. He does not come to condemn, but to show us our blindness so that we might embrace His healing and receive sight. And He often accomplishes this by questions, unsettled hearts, and sometimes through those we have labeled heretics. Personally, I now consider and even embrace the teachings of people that I previously shunned and criticized.

Honestly, we interpret Scripture based upon what we believe about God and about mankind. Therefore, if our understanding of God's heart is wrong, off base, incomplete, etc., we will likely interpret Scripture within the framework of our misunderstanding. Does that leave us without hope? Of course not. The first step is to understand God's heart toward mankind. This is another work of grace. I have prayed quite faithfully (but not very effectively) over the years. But in the last several years, my prayer for almost anybody in any situation would be "Father, may they have a revelation of your Heart and your Love for them." Interpreting Scripture in light of God's heart is the goal. Therefore, before racing to read more Scripture (which is divinely inspired), ask the Lord to reveal the fullness of His heart. Ask Him to reveal the depths of His love. Take a real risk and ask the Lord the following: "Lord, please reveal to me lies that I believe about You."

## IMPEDIMENTS TO UNDERSTANDING: MISUNDERSTANDING

Religious culture, social culture, and life experiences create an impression of God's heart and nature. Oftentimes, that impression is incorrect. As believers, we often then reinforce the wrong view of God with our religious activities, including how we pray. I want to share an experience when God sovereignly started the process of changing my wrong view of His heart. I was totally unaware of my wrong impression, and I did not pray for better clarity. God just generously and graciously corrected my thinking and ruined my prayer life at the same time. As a homeschool family, we were part of a Yahoo group for sharing information. Being a part of the group provided a little extra feeling of connection among homeschool families in the Tri-Cities area.

In December 2009, there was a tragedy in the homeschool community that we heard about on the Yahoo group. Two mothers were returning from shopping when a tree fell on their van killing both of them instantly. They had eight and nine children, respectively. The freak accident was unbelievable but the depth of hurt and pain in their families and in their local congregation was unfathomable. Diane and I were in bed, and even though we did not know either family, we were praying for them. I prayed, "Lord, will you please comfort the families?"

I had no more than uttered those words when I heard God speak to my heart so clearly and say, "You can pray that if you want, but by praying that, it shows that you do not know My heart very well. I am the God of all comfort, and I will always be with them and comfort them." I realized that God's heart meant that He was already comforting, and that He was not waiting on me or anyone else to activate His comforting mode. It cut to the core of what I thought about God—that He has to be primed or convinced to be kind, comforting, loving, or forgiving. And that was the way I had always prayed; endeavoring to convince God to be more benevolent and loving. Of course, that left me speechless, and I did not know what to pray. But it revealed to me that I had greatly misunderstood God's heart. It was an invitation to know His heart and nature more accurately, and I accepted that invitation. It began a process that started very slowly, like a locomotive starting to move from a stationary position, but it has picked up steam over the years and is now increasing exponentially.

When by God's grace I became aware of God's heart of love, kindness, and compassion for me and all humanity, Scripture began to explode in meaning, unlike it ever had before. I began to process and judge everything through a different (and hopefully clearer) lens of God's heart. In the past, we used Scripture to form our views about God. I believe God is willing to share His heart with us and then invites us to interpret and understand Scripture in light of who He is. As an example, when faced with an enemy of myself, an enemy of my friends, or an enemy of the Gospel, I used to pray Biblically from Psalm 35:1 "Contend, LORD, with those who contend with me; fight against those who fight against me." I assigned a meaning that if God were to contend against my enemies that He would destroy them.

It was exceedingly Biblical, but it was not Christlike. It was not initiated by love or compassion, but by a desire for my side to beat their side. It did not reflect God's heart. How did I determine that it did not reflect God's heart? My eyes and heart were open to see how God (rather than David) responds to evil, wicked people. Luke 6:35 "But love your enemies, do good to them, and lend to them without expecting to get anything back. Then your reward will be great, and you will be children of the Most High, *because he is kind to the ungrateful and wicked.*" Did you get that? He is *Kind* to the ungrateful and wicked. God is *Kind*! God is *Kind* to the wicked. I had missed this message of God's kindness for decades while embracing a different message that God is ready to destroy the wicked and His enemies. And if He is willing to destroy His enemies, then He is likely willing to destroy my enemies. Just like me, you may have also missed the message of God's goodness and kindness.

Jesus says that He came that we might have life and might have it more abundantly. He doesn't say that He came so we could be free from sin. Although God does indeed forgive our sins and free us from the power of sin so that we can have an abundant life,

His focus and His laid-down life were not just to erase sin. This will be discussed more thoroughly in a later chapter.

What has the Lord revealed to me about God's heart and God's nature, which I apply to interpret Scripture? The following are the essential, foundational, and absolute characteristics of God and His heart and nature that guide His every action: God is Love, God is kind, God is good, and God has never and will never leave us or separate from us. These have become my absolutes. I will not die on most hills, but I will die on these hills, as I think everything in the Gospel flows from these truths. The Scripture confirms these attributes of God and provides a beautiful basis to interpret the Good News in light of God's attributes.

## GOD IS LOVE!

Undisputedly, God is Love! "The one who does not love does not know God, because God is love. [16]We have come to know and have believed the love which God has [in] us. God is love, and the one who remains in love remains in God, and God remains in him" (1 John 4:8, 16). No Christian disputes that God is Love in his/her theology, but we often endeavor to temper it. And on occasion, we simply do not actually believe it, notwithstanding our professed theology. Ironically, I have found that my theology has often been in conflict with my actual belief system. Our theology is often nothing more than a statement about what we acquiesce to intellectually, and too often provides an invalid justification not to deal with our internal inconsistencies. But God is working graciously. The nature of God's Love is that it loves those whom we perceive as being unlovable, as well as those who feel unlovable. However, we often actually believe just the opposite—that God cannot or will not love the person whom we perceive as unlovable, and we also believe that God cannot love us when we feel unlovable. But in the Kingdom and in God's accurate perception, there are no unlovable people; only misperceptions that certain people are unlovable. Jesus explains to us that even sinners can love those who love them (Luke 6:32-33). If God simply loved us because we were lovable, that would not be any different from the way sinners act. God loves those whom we perceive as unlovable.

The ontological Truth of God is that He is Love, not simply that He acts lovingly. His every fiber of being and thought is Love. Love dictates everything He says, thinks, or does. God's very essence and every response is Love. Because Love is His nature and His being, and because God is completely holy and righteous (because His doing is completely and always consistent with His being), it is impossible for God (the Father, Son, and Holy Spirit) to ever act in any way other than in Love. His only and every motivation for everything is Love. When God extends grace, His Love motivates His grace. When God extends mercy, His Love motivates His mercy. When God is just and promotes justice, His Love motivates His justice. When God extends wrath, His Love motivates His wrath!

But wait, I thought his holiness motivated His wrath, or perhaps His anger motivated His wrath. If God's wrath were motivated by anything other than His Love, then God would be subject to conflicting motivations; the motivation toward wrath would compete against—and have to be greater or stronger than—the motivation of His Love in order for God to move in wrath. That would mean He is not always acting totally out of Love and is thereby experiencing an internal inconsistency. If you think God's Love conflicts with God's holiness, you mistakenly see God like a human who struggles with internal conflict. Simply stated, God is not like us. God acts differently from us and is always internally consistent with Love. When we are wrathful, it is in spite of love. When God acts out of wrath, it is because of His Love, not in spite of it. His wrath is entirely and completely loving. Therefore, I have come to understand and believe that everything God does is only and always motivated by His Love. God always acts in Love! Therefore, for me, the first application of Scriptural interpretation is the foundational truth that God is not only Love, but that God always acts and responds in Love. If you cannot find God's heart of Love in the interpretation of Scripture, you need to take it back to the Spirit of Truth.

IMPEDIMENTS TO UNDERSTANDING: MISUNDERSTANDING

## GOD LOVES YOU!

The theological belief that God is Love must also become a personal revelation that God loves you no matter what you have done and no matter your relationship with Him. It is not enough to view Him as an impersonal God who loves in an abstract way, and it is not enough to view Him as God who generally loves mankind. This beautiful revelation must also be received and applied personally. Even Jesus had this personal revelation of the Father's Love before He began his ministry. "And behold, a voice from the heavens said, 'This is My beloved Son, with whom I am well pleased,'" (Matthew 3:17). Jesus did not start His ministry to become a beloved Son. Jesus received the truth that He was a Beloved Son, and that truth empowered His life and His ministry.

Do you know how much God loves you? Does it seem heretical to say that God loves you as much as He loves Billy Graham or the Apostle John? But even that comparison is insufficient to express the depths of His Love. God loves you and me just as much as He loves Jesus. "I in them and You in Me, that they may be perfected in unity, so that the world may know that You sent Me, and *You loved them, just as You loved Me*" (John 17:23). This assurance and declaration of love is not conditional and applies to everyone—even those who do not believe, and even those who reject His Love.

God's Love is the most powerful transformative force in the world. For generations, followers of Christ have substituted effort toward following the law and commandments in order to facilitate transformation, in place of living from His Love. We often feared that love would not have the power to compel obedience, when in fact it is the most powerful force to empower thankfulness, gratitude, transformation, and obedience. As a result of substituting effort for receiving love, we have focused on law, commandment, and punishment to try to elicit change and transformation. Law and commandment—and the fear that arise from them—may produce changed outward behavior, but they are devoid of the power to bring inner transformation. There is power that can bring inner transformation—God's magnificent, unconditional, unwavering, unearned, never-ending Love.

We condemn ourselves because we should love God more, but loving Him begins by first receiving His Love for us. What if Revelation 2:4 "that you have left your first love," is more about forgetting or failing to receive or live in God's Love that you first received, than about the traditional interpretation and application? First means the beginning or foremost. "We love, because He first loved us" (1 John 4:19). What if we are forgetting His first, amazing Love for us! We can only love because we receive His Love first. Rather than working to love Him more or better, maybe we need to recall, remember, and receive His tremendous Love for us, and once we receive His Love, the natural response is to love Him in return.

In modern Christianity, the invitation to receive God's Love has been deemphasized or minimized by first focusing—and by sometimes solely focusing—on the obligation to love God with all your heart, soul, mind, and strength. Who hasn't been moved by Mark 12:28–31 to make a commitment to love God more and better?

> One of the scribes came up and heard them arguing, and recognizing that He had answered them well, asked Him, "What commandment is the foremost of all?" ²⁹Jesus answered, "The foremost is, 'HEAR, ISRAEL! THE LORD IS OUR GOD, THE LORD IS ONE; ³⁰AND YOU SHALL LOVE THE LORD YOUR GOD WITH ALL YOUR HEART, AND WITH ALL YOUR SOUL, AND WITH ALL YOUR MIND, AND WITH ALL YOUR STRENGTH.' ³¹The second is this: 'YOU SHALL LOVE YOUR NEIGHBOR AS YOURSELF.' There is no other commandment greater than these."

After hearing this recited and preached, we often commit (and recommit) to the obligation without first receiving His Love, which is the power to love Him in return. I believe this passage has been interpreted and applied in a legalistic, earning, or performance approach rather than in a grace-filled receiving approach. There is no way for any of us to love the Lord with all our heart, soul, mind, and strength unless we have first received God's Love for our whole heart, our whole soul, our whole mind, and our whole strength. Let God love your entirety, and then your entirety can love God, but your entirety cannot love God until your entirety first receives God's Love. With God, receiving His Love always comes before giving love. Our focus has been backwards, and it has handicapped us.

I could send you out to follow this instruction to love God more with your whole heart, soul, and strength. But if I challenge you to love God more without inviting you to first receive more of God's Love for you, I will leave you ill-equipped and will only frustrate you. In addition, you would likely be frustrated because you have already tried that, and you did not feel that it worked. Let's look back at the scribe's question. "Which is the greatest law, or which commandment is the foremost?" He was asking a question about the law, and Jesus answered the question that the scribe asked. But we are not under the law; we are under the Gospel of grace. So there is another question that is appropriate—"Under the Gospel of grace, what is the greatest invitation?"

We love only when we first learn how to receive the Love of the Father. "The one who does not love does not know God, because God is love" (1 John 4:8). Stated another way, the one who does not love does not know Love or is not living loved. What is the key to loving God? "We love, because He first loved us" (1 John 4:19). Life does not change because we begin to love God with all our heart, soul, mind, and strength. Life changes when we begin to receive God's magnificent, unconditional, unwavering, unearned, never-ending Love for us; for every part of our heart, soul, mind, and strength, and then there is no other possible response but thankfulness and to return love.

## GOD IS KIND!

God is also kind. He is never not kind. He is not only kind to the believers; He is kind to the unbelievers. He is never unkind. Luke 6:35 "But love your enemies and do good, and lend, expecting nothing in return; and your reward will be great, and you will be sons of the Most High; *for He Himself is kind to ungrateful and evil people.*" Because He is Love and always acts in Love, it is impossible for God to ever be unkind.

1 Corinthians 13:4 reminds us that love is kind. Because God is Love, then 1 Corinthians 13 must be describing God! What if 1 Corinthians 13 is especially a description of how God acts and responds toward us rather than only a description of how we are supposed to act and treat others? Because God is Love, I will substitute God for Love, which is a Biblically sound exercise, to make my point. "⁴God is patient, God is kind, God is not jealous; God does not brag, God is not arrogant. ⁵God does not act disgracefully, God does not seek its own benefit; God is not provoked, God does not keep an account of a wrong, ⁶God does not rejoice in unrighteousness, but rejoices with the truth;⁷God keeps every confidence, God believes all things, God hopes all things, God endures all things." I wholeheartedly embrace this description of God.

Furthermore, what if 1 Corinthians 13 is a description of how we live and react when Christ is living through us? How could our expressed love ever be kind if God was not first kind to us? And He is kind, always and forever. Romans 2:4 "Or do you think lightly of the riches of His kindness and restraint and patience, not knowing that the kindness of God leads you to repentance?" There has never been a time when God was not kind! There will never be a time when God is not kind!

His responses to us are always kind. Let's take an example of Jesus's interaction with people whose faith falters to show how He responds with gentleness and kindness. If anyone should have been forever convinced that Jesus was the Messiah, it would have been John the Baptist. He undoubtedly knew the story of his miraculous conception. He actually saw himself prophesied about in relation to the Messiah in Isaiah. When he baptized Jesus, he heard God's own voice from heaven declare that Jesus was His beloved Son. He received such an amazing confirmation of both his purpose and that Jesus is the Messiah that he should never again doubt that Jesus was the Messiah. And then just a few months after John baptized

Jesus, while he's in prison, he questions the word that he received, and he questions whether Jesus really was the Messiah. He probably thought, *"Would the real Messiah really leave me sitting here in the prison?" "If He is the Messiah, wouldn't He deliver me?"* We are very similar to John. Our prisons, struggles, and disappointments have a way of causing us to question what we previously thought to be certain. However, no one needs convincing that we fall back into doubt and unbelief at times. I shared all of this in order to share Jesus's kind and gentle response to John when John stops believing. Jesus was gentle in His response; He encouraged, He did not condemn, judge, or become angry with John. He understood. Jesus responded in exactly the same way with Thomas. John 20:27 "Then He said to Thomas, 'Place your finger here, and see My hands; and take your hand and put it into My side; and do not continue in disbelief, but be a believer.'" And this is exactly the same way He responds to us when we doubt or cannot seem to believe; He never condemns, judges, or becomes angry; rather, He encourages us in belief because He is gentle and kind.

## GOD IS GOOD!

"God is good all the time, and all the time God is good." Is this really true or just a cliche'? Now let's look at God's attribute as good. "So if you, despite being evil, know how to give good gifts to your children, how much more will your Father who is in heaven give good things to those who ask Him!" (Matthew 7:11).

"But Jesus said to him, 'Why do you call Me good? No one is good except God alone,'" (Mark 10:13). (See also Luke 18:19.) Jesus was not saying that He was not good, because as God He was indeed good, being of the same substance as the Father (which is further discussed below). He was posing a question to the gentleman to ask him *if* the reason the gentleman thought He was good was because He was God. Jesus was challenging the man's belief system as to whether Jesus was inherently good based upon His being or whether he had obtained goodness by His actions. Jesus was challenging the gentleman to conclude that, as God, it would be impossible for Him to be anything other than good. Do you believe that it is impossible for God to be anything other than good? Does your theology or interpretation of Scripture allow you to believe otherwise?

Jesus is not only good in concept or theologically, but His goodness is expressed as the Good Shepherd who cares for His sheep. We are well aware from Psalm 23 that the Lord God is our shepherd, but we must never forget that the Lord God is a good, good shepherd. "I am the good shepherd; the good shepherd lays down His life for the sheep" (John 10:11). And it is His goodness that leads us to repentance. Nevertheless, we often subconsciously conclude that Jesus is good, but the Father is not so good, maybe even angry and wrathful. Of course, the Father ends up forgiving us, but we have been taught that Jesus had to be cruelly crucified so that the Father could have legal grounds to forgive us. Assigning roles as good cop and bad cop sometimes seems like the only way to resolve the apparent conflict when we were taught that God required Jesus's crucifixion in order to forgive our sins. But Love never requires a payment in order to forgive, and neither does the Godhead. For those who have contemplated and tried to resolve this conflict, I first honor you for not suppressing the struggle. I honor you that you are seeing the story as inconsistent with the nature of God. This will be developed in more detail below, but because God is Love and is good, you will see that the story that Scripture actually writes is that God chose to forgive all of us without the requirement of a substitutionary sacrifice. That truth removes a huge obstacle that has rightly hindered many of you from really embracing the truth that God is good.

If you are a parent, you have learned that the hardest question to provide an understandable response to your child is a "why" question. Why questions are not necessarily hard to answer, just hard for a child with limited understanding and limited life experiences to understand or perceive. But we ask God "why" questions all the time and often demand to know and understand. Every time we ask a "why" question about God or to God, if we do not begin with the foundational belief and trust that He is good, kind, and loving, we risk getting the wrong answer because we begin with the wrong assumption about His heart and His character. In our longing to understand situations, we construct a logical or reasonable response, but our response may misrepresent God and His heart. God is indeed always and in every circumstance good.

He is so good that it is impossible for God to do anything in response to our failures or unbelief other than to cause them to work together for our good (Romans 8:28). Causing all things to work together for our good is not a result of God's analysis or reasoned decision in a particular situation to turn it to good. God is not discretionary with regard to whether to turn a situation to good. God does not decide that some failures will work for our good, but others will not. Causing all failures to work for our good is a result of His nature and His being, which are always good. Because He is good, the fruit or response that comes from Him when we fail must, without exception, be good. It may seem funny, but I learned something about the redemptive nature of God when I failed at playing Wordle.

I started playing Wordle in July 2022. Wordle is a word game in which you get six chances to guess a five-letter word. There are more than 158,000 five-letter words in the English language. What are the chances of guessing the right word in just six attempts? Well, actually much better than you may expect. In more than three years, there have been fewer than ten times that I did not guess the word. Given the probabilities, how do we explain my success, or your success if you play Wordle? It is pretty simple; only the first guess is a blind guess. Subsequent guesses are not in isolation from the prior guesses. Subsequent guesses build on what you got correct, but subsequent guesses also learn from what you got wrong. Learning from an incorrect guess is what enables the ability to correctly guess the word in six or fewer attempts. This process is similar to life and especially similar to the Kingdom of God. In the Kingdom and in the Gospel, God graciously takes "what we get wrong" and uses it to lead us to greater truth about Him and about ourselves. The goal is not to never "get it wrong." The goal is not even to never "sin." If that were the goal, Jesus would have told

Peter to go home and lock himself in his house so that he would not deny Jesus three times, so that Peter would have avoided the mistake of denying Jesus. The goal is to know God. Jesus describes eternal life as knowing God (John 17:3). How beautiful that "when I get it wrong," God nevertheless uses it and enables me to know Him even more completely. Now that's a good, kind, grace-giving, loving God.

## GOD HAS NEVER AND WILL NEVER SEPARATE FROM US!

God has never been absent from us; God will never be absent from us; God could never be absent from us. God never turns away from us. He will never leave us or forsake us. Hebrews 13:5 "He Himself has said, 'I WILL NEVER DESERT YOU, NOR WILL I EVER ABANDON YOU.'" God is not afraid of sin. God is not allergic to sin. He doesn't have a reaction to sin or to being around sin. He does not have to stay away from the unclean. For generations, Christians have held and proclaimed that because God is holy, He cannot stand in the presence of sin. I taught this consistently, but then I began to understand that this is inconsistent with the nature of Love, and it is totally different from what Jesus modeled for us. Jesus never separated from sinners. In fact, He was drawn to them. He mingled with them. He ate with them. As established from the Old Covenant Levitical laws, certain people were "unclean" because of their physical condition, including lepers and women who were in their menstrual cycle.

In the Old Covenant, if a person touched an "unclean" person, the clean person became "unclean." But with Jesus's ministry (which moved from law to grace and truth), Jesus approached and touched the "unclean" person, and rather than causing Jesus to become "unclean," the "unclean" person was healed and made clean. Jesus did not have to avoid or distance Himself from the physically or the spiritually "unclean." And Jesus and the Father are not different, although Christians have often thought of Jesus as being

## IMPEDIMENTS TO UNDERSTANDING: MISUNDERSTANDING

kind and loving and the Father as being wrathful and judgmental. Actually, Jesus and the Father are identical.

Looking at Jesus and Philip's interaction in John 14:8-9 gives great insight. "Philip said to Him, 'Lord, show us the Father, and it is enough for us.' ⁹Jesus said to him, 'Have I been with you for so long a time, and yet you have not come to know Me, Philip? The one who has seen Me has seen the Father; how can you say, "Show us the Father?"' In Jesus's own words, He describes Himself and the Father as one and the same. Sounds like they are mirror images of one another which we find to be further supported by Colossians 1:15, 19 "He is the image of the invisible God, the firstborn of all creation: ¹⁹For it was the Father's good pleasure for all the fullness to dwell in Him," and Hebrews 1:3 "And He is the radiance of His glory and the exact representation of His nature, and upholds all things by the word of His power. When He had made purification of sins, He sat down at the right hand of the Majesty on high." Scripture is clear and direct that Jesus and the Father are the same in every regard. "For in Him all the fullness of Deity dwells in bodily form" (Colossians 2:9). And when we see Jesus acting and responding to the "unclean" and "sinners," let's not forget that He was only saying what He heard His Father say, and He was only doing what He saw His Father doing.

What he did and said reflected exactly the heart of the Father because they are exactly the same. Jesus never acted inconsistently with the Father's heart. When we see Jesus loving and healing, we see the Father loving and healing. "For I did not speak on My own, but the Father Himself who sent Me has given Me a commandment as to what to say and what to speak" (John 12:49). "Therefore Jesus answered and was saying to them, 'Truly, truly, I say to you, the Son can do nothing of Himself, unless it is something He sees the Father doing; for whatever the Father does, these things the Son also does in the same way'" (John 5:19).

But there are two Bible passages on which we have based our mistaken belief that God separates from sin and sinners. If we are going to truly believe and receive that God has never separated from us, we have to wrestle with these passages. One is the story of

Adam and Eve, and one is Jesus on the cross. One false narrative is easily corrected by looking directly at the story and language, while the other false narrative is more entrenched in our view of God. Let's look at them separately.

I was taught that after Adam and Eve ate of the forbidden fruit from the tree of knowledge of good and evil, God turned away from them. It was actually just the opposite. Adam and Eve turned away and endeavored to hide from the Presence of God. What, however, was God's reaction to the introduction of sin into humanity? God moves toward the sin and the sinners. Genesis 3:8-9 "Now they heard the sound of the LORD God walking in the garden in the cool of the day, and the man and his wife hid themselves from the presence of the LORD God among the trees of the garden. ⁹Then the LORD God called to the man, and said to him, 'Where are you?'"

When Jesus is on the cross, Matthew and Mark record the following: "And about the ninth hour Jesus cried out with a loud voice, saying, 'ELI, ELI, LEMA SABAKTANEI?' that is, 'MY GOD, MY GOD, WHY HAVE YOU FORSAKEN ME?'" (Matthew 27:46). We have been taught that God could not look on Jesus who became sin. Doesn't this single verse confirm that God must distance Himself from sin? From Jesus's own mouth, we hear that the Father turned away from Him. But what of the promises of Hebrews 13:5 or Psalm 139:8 "If I ascend to heaven, You are there; If I make my bed in Sheol, behold, You are there?" Are these promises only an allegory, but not a reality? How can we harmonize a belief that God turns away from sin and sinners with Romans 8:38-39 "For I am convinced that neither death, nor life, nor angels, nor principalities, nor things present, nor things to come, nor powers, ³⁹nor height, nor depth, nor any other created thing will be able to separate us from the love of God that is in Christ Jesus our Lord?" Can we be separated from God or not? Will God separate from us?

Jesus recites the first line of Psalm 22 when on the cross, but it was not a theological statement. It was actually a declaration of faith to the entirety of Psalm 22, and especially Psalm 22:24 ("For He has not despised nor scorned the suffering of the afflicted; *Nor has He hidden His face from him*; But when he cried to Him for help, He heard.") Jesus was declaring that even when it felt like God had forsaken Him, He believed the truth and the promise made by the Godhead before creation that God would never forsake Him and that God would never hide His face from Him. Jesus became man with the promise and assurance that God would never separate from Him, that God would never leave Him, that God would never forsake Him. Before Jesus went to the cross, He had this eternal promise from the Godhead. He knew in advance that He would have to rely on this promise when it did not feel true. In his conversation with the disciples which is recorded in John 16:32, Jesus is looking ahead by the Spirit and declaring that He will rely on this promise when He is on the Cross: "Behold, an hour is coming, and has already come, for you to be scattered, each to his own home, and to leave Me alone; and yet I am not alone, because the Father is with Me." Jesus's strength was in the fact that He knew He would never, ever be alone, although He felt alone. He had a promise from God that God would never forsake Him. This is the same promise that God has made to each of us.

This is profound because Jesus, as the Second Man and the Last Adam, had to be tempted with everything with which mankind would be tempted.[1] One of the temptations which we often face is a false belief that God has forsaken us or that God will forsake us. Our customary response to failure is that God has forsaken us, because we often believe that our obedience keeps us in good standing with a fickle God. Therefore, we often think and live like God has separated from us, but He never has and never will. But we are tempted to believe that, often and repeatedly. The Godhead knew that mankind would be tempted to believe this lie, that God has forsaken me, and according to Hebrews 4:15, Jesus, as the Second Man, but the perfect man, had to struggle for the truth in the midst of circumstantial uncertainty. ("For we do not have a

---

1. Hebrews 2:17 "Therefore, in all things He had to be made like His brothers so that He might become a merciful and faithful high priest in things pertaining to God, to make propitiation for the sins of the people."

high priest who cannot sympathize with our weaknesses, but One who has been tempted in all things just as we are, yet without sin.")

Jesus's circumstances cast doubt on the truth that He knew and upon the promise that the Godhead made before the incarnation, and He held on to the truth, knowing that God would not forsake Him. Because Jesus's life is an example and first fruit of the life we can live in Christ, He had to experience the darkness of the emotions that God had left Him, but by referencing Psalm 22 He actually declared that God had not hidden His face from Him although it certainly felt like it. Jesus sets the example of living by every word that proceeds from God's mouth rather than by feelings. Therefore, his recitation of Psalm 22 was actually a statement of faith and belief in the midst of contrary emotions. He was declaring again what he had earlier told to His disciples that "He was not alone."

Even more importantly, where was God when Jesus was on the cross? Was He hiding His face? He absolutely was not! God was in Christ; God was with Christ. This is profoundly important. "Namely, that *God was in Christ* reconciling the world to Himself, not counting their wrongdoings against them, and He has committed to us the word of reconciliation" (2 Corinthians 5:19). I know this messes with our certainty and our linear distinction between each member of the Godhead, but it could not be more clear. Jesus was not alone on the cross; the Father and the Holy Spirit (God) were in Christ. They had not forsaken Him at all; they remained in and with Jesus.

God the Father, God the Son, and God the Holy Spirit have always been connected in perfect unity, interconnectedness, mutual submission, and interdependence. If Calvary, the cross, and Jesus taking upon His body the sin of the world (1 Peter 2:24) could create a fracture or separation between the Godhead, Satan knew it would be a victory because he understood that the Godhead eternally existed in perfect unity. Satan had seen this perfect unity modeled and lived out. He knew the power of the Godhead functioned through complete and perfect unity. Even if Jesus paid for all the sins of the world, but the Godhead suffered separation,

Satan would claim victory because the power of the Godhead is exhibited in and exists from unity and connectedness. The common thought that the Cross is mostly about sin removal rather than about restored relationship, restored fellowship, and constant connection may hinder us from understanding how destructive separation among the Godhead would have been. Love is the power and strength of the Godhead's unity, and if unity is broken, that means that Love is also broken. If separation in the Godhead occurs, that means Love has failed. Unity could only be lost at the cost of Love failing. "In addition to all these things love, which is the perfect bond of unity," or literally "the uniting bond of perfection" (Colossians 3:14).

Satan endeavored to use sin or choice to separate in the garden. However, God came to Adam and Eve in their sin rather than separating from them. But Adam and Eve were just two individuals. Could the Godhead really withstand all of the sin nature of all mankind heaped upon the Son of God? How would it be possible for that situation not to separate the Father (who is holy) and the Holy Spirit (who is holy) from Jesus, the Lamb (who had been defiled by all the sin of the world)? And that was Satan's hope from the cross and crucifixion: that the Father or Holy Spirit would turn away from the defiled One. But rather than separate, the Father and the Holy Spirit abided with Jesus, even to the darkest regions of hell. (2 Corinthians 5:19 "Namely, that God was in Christ reconciling the world to Himself, not counting their wrongdoings against them, and He has committed to us the word of reconciliation.") And this proves that sin does not have the power to separate Jesus from God on the cross, and further proves that sin does not have the power to separate us from God. This is indeed the crux of the Good News. It is a central element of the Gospel.

I think Satan's goal of broken unity is the same reason Satan tempted Jesus to turn the stones into bread. In the wilderness, Satan tempted Jesus three times. Each of the temptations had the possibility of destroying God's plan. If Jesus had succumbed to any of the three temptations, Satan would have defeated the Godhead. But why did Satan tempt Jesus to turn stones into bread to eat?

Bread is not evil. Eating is not evil. It was not that turning stone into bread was evil or sin, but that doing so would result in Jesus acting independently from the Father, rather than being dependent upon Him. Jesus would have done something that He had not heard the Father say. Isn't it interesting that Satan recognized the power in this temptation? If Jesus had succumbed to this temptation, it would have been equivalent to or had the same consequences as Jesus succumbing to the temptation to bow down and worship Satan in exchange for all the kingdoms of the world. Satan's plan was to separate Jesus from the Father by tempting Him to ignore the Father's voice and live in independence. Because the Godhead has always lived in perfect unity and will always live in perfect unity, interconnectedness, mutual submission, and interdependence, it would have fractured the Godhead if Jesus acted independently of God, and it also would have fractured the Godhead if God turned away from Jesus on the Cross. And it would defy Love for the Godhead to turn away from you in your sin or brokenness.

And one more shocker before we move on. Referring to Revelation 14:10 ("He also will drink of the wine of the wrath of God, which is mixed in full strength in the cup of His anger; and he will be tormented with fire and brimstone in the presence of the holy angels *and in the presence of the Lamb*"), the place of fire and brimstone is actually in the presence of God, not away from it. It is worth noting that Greek Orthodox theology holds that the lake of fire is the holy and purifying presence of God's Love. In fact, Hebrews 12:29 tells us that "our God is a consuming God," or stated differently, "Love is a consuming God." God's fire is always redemptive, He is always present in the fire, and God's fire is always motivated by Love. God's presence with and rescuing of Shadrach, Meshach, and Abednego, who were thrown into the middle of the furnace of blazing fire by King Nebuchadnezzar, are a foreshadowing of this truth. "'Look! I see four men untied and walking about in the middle of the fire unharmed, and the appearance of the fourth is like a son of the gods!'" (Daniel 3:25). God was in the fire with them. In addition to protecting them from being consumed by the fire, God also freed them from being bound. His presence

## IMPEDIMENTS TO UNDERSTANDING: MISUNDERSTANDING

is with us to work redemption and salvation into the heart of all mankind. God simply cannot separate or disconnect from us. It is spiritually and righteously impossible for God to separate or disconnect from us. He never has. He never will.

If you have to change the attributes or nature of God so that He is not always good, kind, and loving, in order to offer an explanation of why God interacts with humanity in a certain way, you need to re-examine your belief. When I have an understanding of Scripture that contradicts one of these non-negotiable attributes, that God is Love, that God is kind, that God is good, and that God never separates or hides from us, then I will back up and ask the Lord to show me the truth about the Scripture that I am missing. The simple truth is that when we read and interpret Scripture based upon a false understanding of God's attributes and nature, we will use Scripture to further validate our false beliefs about God and the Gospel. However, once I had a more accurate understanding of God's attributes, God's character, and God's nature, the beauty of the Good News opened up like a beautiful flower in the morning dew. I believe it will for you, too!

# Chapter 3

## Impediments to Understanding the Full Message of the Gospel
*Terminology*

ANOTHER IMPEDIMENT TO UNDERSTANDING the Gospel is to misunderstand the Greek meaning of Biblical terms as they were used and understood by the writers of the New Testament. My wife, Diane, grew up in Minnesota. She received her BSN degree in Minnesota and did her clinicals in St. Paul. When she graduated, unionized RNs in Minnesota were striking, there was violence, and nursing jobs were cloaked with uncertainty. Rather than cross the picket lines, Diane and Ann (her best friend from the third grade) decided to go out of state, get experience, and return to Minnesota in a couple of years. (By the way, this plan did not work out like Diane expected, but it sure worked out well for me as I met Diane in Big Stone Gap, Virginia, just as she was contemplating returning to Minnesota.)

Diane and Ann moved to Wise, Virginia, and worked for a very small rural hospital in the Appalachian Healthcare System, which subsequently closed. Moving from metropolitan Minneapolis to Wise was a culture shock for them in every way. But practically, the language barrier was most problematic. While their accents were different, of course, the bigger dilemma was the utilization of words. It left Diane and Ann completely confused. For instance, a nurse would tell a patient "to mash" the button if the patient needed anything. Instantly, Diane was envisioning mashing something destructively, perhaps with a hammer, as if to destroy it. Diane was thinking to herself, "Why would you mash and destroy the button?" Diane would have instructed the patient to push the button. There were numerous examples of this language barrier, and eventually Diane and Ann figured out the vocabulary. The point is that they had the same intention, but they used different language, which created confusion. They were not on the same page. This also often happens with Biblical terminology.

## DIFFERENTIATING BETWEEN REDEMPTION, JUSTIFICATION, AND SALVATION

Unfortunately, in our Christian culture, there tends to be a language barrier where some Biblical terms are misunderstood, and some are mistakenly used interchangeably. Until my late 30s, I understood and used the Biblical terms justification, righteous, righteousness, redemption, salvation, saved, and sanctification interchangeably. I considered each of these words a synonym for the others. As one should expect, there are distinct meanings for each of them, and ascribing the same general meaning results in Scriptures that are confusing, a confused interpretation of Scripture, and ultimately a confusing Gospel. All of the elements of the Kingdom of God convey a different idea. When you lump them all into a general category, you limit the value of each of them. A penny, a nickel, a dime, a quarter, a dollar, a five-dollar bill, a ten-dollar bill, a twenty-dollar bill, a fifty-dollar bill, and a hundred-dollar bill are all currency. Imagine if you did not distinguish one from the other. We have done this with these beautiful terms.

Nowhere is this more detrimental to receiving the full message of the Gospel than with the use of the term "saved." "Are you saved?" "When were you saved?" Jesus, John, Peter, and Paul used the word "save" in a completely different context from our current religious language. In essence, the post-Reformation church has changed the meaning of "saved" or "salvation" to be something different from how it is used in Scripture. That can be overcome if you are on the same page; however, we are often speaking a different language, but do not realize it. The resulting consequence is that we read "save" or "saved" or "salvation" in Scripture and ascribe to it a different meaning than the writer intended. Therefore, it is impossible to correctly understand or interpret the Scripture in light of the incorrect meaning. Utilizing the form of "save" in this manner is inconsistent with the Greek meaning and utilization. That often means when we read the words "saved" and "salvation" in Scripture, that we are actually thinking in terms of our evolved and adapted definition like "Have you been saved?" or "Are you going to heaven when you die?" rather than the definition which Jesus, John, Peter, and Paul would have contemplated; we are comparing apples and oranges.

The Greek word for salvation is "soteria." It means "deliverance, preservation, and salvation." It does not mean and has never meant "to have prayed the sinner's prayer," and it has never meant "to accept Jesus's provision for the forgiveness of sins." Salvation is most similar to sanctification. Sanctification means *the process* of taking the defiled or common and making it holy or setting it apart. It cannot be accomplished without someone separating himself or withdrawing from fellowship with the world. It requires participation on our behalf. Therefore, this is a process achieved by "withdrawal from fellowship with the world and from selfishness by first gaining fellowship with God and toward God." Although there are common elements among them, salvation is not justification or redemption.

Our redemption is a *divine one-time established provision* from God to and for you out of His abundant Grace. None of us asked the Godhead to provide redemption. None of us has the power to negate the power of redemption. This *divine provision* was decreed before creation, was fulfilled from the creation of the world (Revelation 13:8 "... the Lamb who was slain from the creation of the world"), was expressed within the confines of time

## IMPEDIMENTS TO UNDERSTANDING: TERMINOLOGY

at Calvary, and has everlasting and eternal consequences in the universe. Notwithstanding the eternal, on-going consequences, Jesus was crucified once, as we see from Hebrews 9:12 and 24–26[1], and by the shedding of His blood, provided redemption for all of mankind. Ephesians 1:7: "In him we have redemption through his blood, the forgiveness of sins, in accordance with the riches of God's grace that he lavished on us with all wisdom and understanding." (See Colossians 1:13–14; 1 Timothy 2:5-6; 1 John 2:2 and 4:10, 1 Peter 1:18–19, and Romans 3:22(b)-25.)[2]

Justification, which means "to make one righteous, as if you never sinned," is only a part of redemption. We will talk more about how this occurs, but for now, justification (forgiveness of

---

1. Hebrews 9:12 He did not enter by means of the blood of goats, and calves; but he entered the Most Holy Place *once for all by his own blood, having obtained eternal redemption.*

Hebrews 9:24—26 For Christ did not enter a holy place made by hands, a mere copy of the true one, but into heaven itself, now to appear in the presence of God for us; [25]*nor was it that He would offer Himself often,* as the high priest enters the Holy Place year by year with blood that is not his own. [26]Otherwise, He would have needed to suffer often since the foundation of the world; but now once at the consummation of the ages He has been revealed to put away sin by the sacrifice of Himself.

Note: There is a significance to the fact that Jesus was revealed to "put away sin" as opposed to "put away sins" which we will discuss later.

2. Colossians 1:13—14 For he has rescued us from the dominion of darkness and brought us into the kingdom of the Son he loves, in whom we have redemption, the forgiveness of sins.

1 Timothy 2:5—6 For there is one God and one mediator between God and men, the man Jesus Christ, who gave himself as a ransom for all men . . . .

1 John 2:2 and He Himself is the propitiation for our sins; and not for ours only, but also for the sins of the whole world.

1 John 4:10 In this is love, not that we loved God, but that He loved us and sent His Son to be the propitiation for our sins,

1 Peter 1:18—19 For you know that it was not with perishable things such as silver or gold that you were redeemed from the empty way of life handed down to you from your forefathers, but with the precious blood of Christ, a lamb without blemish or defect.

Romans 3:22(b)—25 There is no difference, for all have sinned and fall short of the glory of God, and are justified freely by his grace through the redemption that came by Christ Jesus. God presented him as a sacrifice of atonement, through faith in his blood (NIV).

sins) is available because of the plan of redemption. Justification could therefore be thought of as a divine pronouncement or a divine change of status. You were once guilty of sins, but now you have been justified and made righteous. Simply speaking, you are no longer guilty of sins, which is Good News. Biblically, justification and righteousness are most similar, perhaps the different sides of the same coin. And your righteousness is based upon God's decision, not your actions. Romans 3:24 summarizes it well: *"being justified as a gift by His grace through* the redemption which is in Christ Jesus." Paul reaffirms again in Titus 3:7 that our justification comes from God's grace, not from our actions or efforts: "so that *being justified by His grace* we would be made heirs according to the hope of eternal life."

Having been forgiven of the debt of sins that we could never pay, we now have the opportunity to receive the abundant life that Jesus offered. If we think "forgiveness of sins" and "abundant life" are the same, we will always be confused regarding the process of salvation. After being justified and made righteous, we submit and/or surrender to a process of salvation, which is really receiving and walking in abundant life all the time. Having been justified, you are invited into the process of being saved or sanctified. (See Romans 5:1 and Romans 5:9.) According to the Greek definition, salvation is the process of being transformed into His likeness and image by the renewing of our minds.

Salvation is, therefore, when properly interpreted, a *divine process*. Because it is a process, it is past tense, present tense, and future tense. Salvation could be described as follows: you have been saved, you are being saved, and you will be saved. Justification or being made righteous is always only in the past tense. If you look at Romans 13:11(b) "The hour has come for you to wake up from your slumber, because our salvation is nearer now than when we first believed," and Philippians 2:12 "So then, my beloved, just as you have always obeyed, not as in my presence only, but now much more in my absence, work out your own salvation with fear and trembling," you see that the Scripture allude to "salvation" as an ongoing process rather than a one-time established event. God is faithful and patient in this process for each individual, and having begun a good work in you (justification), He will faithfully and patiently carry it (salvation or sanctification) on until its completion in you (Philippians 1:6).

Justification comes first; then the process of salvation begins. Romans 5:9–10 "Since we have now been justified by his blood, how much more shall we be saved from God's wrath through him! For if, when we were God's enemies, we were reconciled[3] to him through the death of his Son, how much more, having been reconciled, shall we be saved through his life!" (NIV). Clearly, we are reconciled first, which creates an opportunity or invitation to submit to the process of salvation. Our reconciliation occurs because God justifies us and makes us righteous, and then His Life is constantly and always available so that we have an abundant life all the time, every day. Our soul and our daily living, our daily walk, is being saved to an abundant life.

Understanding the various Greek meanings of redemption, justification, and salvation will enable you to more accurately understand Scripture as you embrace the full message of this new life.

## DIFFERENTIATING THE KINGDOM OF GOD FROM HEAVEN

I used to believe that the Kingdom of God and the Kingdom of Heaven were the opposite of eternal judgment; that you either spent eternity in the Kingdom of Heaven or in hell. But the Kingdom of God or Kingdom of Heaven is not something that we inherit in the future; it is currently reigning in the world and available for those who embrace it and follow Jesus. God's life does not start when we get to heaven. It starts the moment you trust and receive Jesus's life-giving provision. Eternal life isn't a location; it is the person of Jesus, and the Godhead wants you to participate in that life. Jesus described eternal life in John 17:3, and He does not describe it as life after death in heaven, although

---

3. The Greek meaning of reconcile means "to change mutually; to compound a difference; or to reconcile."

it will continue after our natural death. Eternal life is knowing the Father and the Son. "And this is eternal life, that they may know You, the only true God, and Jesus Christ whom You have sent."

When you know the heart of God—that He is Love, that He is kind, that He is good, and that He will never ever leave or forsake you—it produces joy and security, and it alleviates fear. When you live from the Love God has for you, you are living from truth, and it produces joy and security, which is the highest form of living. Colossians 1:13 "For He rescued us from the domain of darkness, and transferred us to the kingdom of His beloved Son." The opposite of the Kingdom of God/Kingdom of Heaven isn't eternal punishment, but darkness. You can live in the world either in darkness or in the Kingdom of Light. For those people who are described as not inheriting the Kingdom of God, this does not mean they are banished to hell, but rather that they failed to live in the life and power of the Kingdom. They are living much lower than their right and their provision. They are living in darkness rather than light. And life is the light of the world. (John 1:4 "In Him was life, and the life was the Light of mankind.")

> "There is a difference, beloved, between the Gospel of grace and the Gospel of the kingdom of heaven. The Gospel of grace introduces us to Jesus. We hear of His sacrifice, His death on the cross, we are assured of a place in heaven. The Gospel of the kingdom includes the amazing news of God's favor, but also brings us into the spiritual reality of heaven. We are born again from above; a new heavenly life, born of the Holy Spirit, beings aligning our hearts with the life and power of heaven. Indeed, as we actually become disciples and study Christ's words, we cannot help but realize: Jesus did not come simply to bring us to heaven when we die; He came to bring heaven to where we live."[4]

In Luke 22:18 Jesus says, "For I say to you, I will not drink of the fruit of the vine from now on until the kingdom of God comes." This was at the Last Supper, and then after the resurrection,

---

4. Frangipane, December 13, 2002.

## IMPEDIMENTS TO UNDERSTANDING: TERMINOLOGY

Jesus cooks breakfast for the disciples, and they eat together (John 21:12-14). And the Kingdom of God had come because it was not a place, but a spiritual dimension (John 18:36). It is the Kingdom of "righteousness, peace and joy" (Romans 14:17) and "not a matter of talk but of power" (1 Corinthians 4:20). Jesus even tells his hearers in Mark 9:1 that they "will not taste death until they see the Kingdom of God when it has come with power." And in answer to the Pharisees in Luke 17:20-21, He states that the Kingdom of God is in their midst. (Luke 17:20-21 "Now He was questioned by the Pharisees as to when the kingdom of God was coming, and He answered them and said, 'The kingdom of God is not coming with signs that can be observed; [21]nor will they say, "Look, here it is!" or, "There it is!" For behold, the kingdom of God is in your midst.'") Lastly, you do not inherit the Kingdom of God by physically dying, but by being born again. John 3:3 "Jesus responded and said to him, 'Truly, truly, I say to you, unless someone is born again, he cannot see the kingdom of God.'"

Jesus makes it pretty clear in Matthew 12:28 that the Kingdom of God had come: "But if I cast out the demons by the Spirit of God [which He did], then the kingdom of God has come upon you." And since the Kingdom of God is power, it empowers us to overcome while living in this world, which Jesus again declares in Matthew 16:19 "I will give you the keys of the kingdom of heaven; and whatever you bind on earth shall have been bound in heaven, and whatever you loose on earth shall have been loosed in heaven."

John 14:2, which reads as follows, "In My Father's house are many rooms; if that were not so, I would have told you, because I am going there to prepare a place for you," has also led to a misunderstanding of the Kingdom of God. As translated, it points to a future benefit rather than a present reality. The translation of this verse communicates that the future is more important than the present and has resulted in many believers simply waiting to be rescued from the present life to take possession of their mansion in heaven.

When we look at the Greek words, the more accurate reading of John 14:2 would be "My Father's house (abode or residence) is composed of many places where they dwell."[5] That means that John 14:2 is actually focused on where God dwells. It is focused on the present rather than what happens after death. And of course, His dwelling place is within us. Therefore, if we understood that John 14:2 is not referring to a mansion in heaven, but rather the corporate interconnected place where God lives in our hearts currently, we would more easily realize that the Kingdom of Heaven is now rather than limiting it to the afterlife. In other words, the house of the Lord is us, which is entirely consistent with John, Ephesians, Hebrews, and 1 Peter.[6] We do not wait until the afterlife for God to make his dwelling place in us; the Kingdom of God or the Kingdom of Heaven is within us now. The Kingdom of God and the Kingdom of Heaven are not something to anticipate after death, but rather something to receive and live in now.

## UNDERSTANDING THE GREEK MEANING OF "REPENT" OR "REPENTANCE"

"Metanoia" is the Greek word for repentance, and "metanoeō" is the Greek word for repent. Metanoia is a noun, and metanoeō is a verb. The verb means "to change one's mind." It does not mean *"to*

---

5. Let's take a closer look at John 14:2 "In My Father's house [oikia—3614] are many rooms [mŏnā—3438]; if that were not so, I would have told you, because I am going there to prepare a place for you." The Greek word "oikia" means a house or dwelling and the Greek word "mŏnā" means staying, abiding, dwelling, abode, to make an (one's) abode.

6. John 14:23 Jesus answered and said to him, "If anyone loves Me, he will follow My word; and My Father will love him, and We will come to him and make Our dwelling [3428] with him.

1 Peter 2:5 You also, like living stones, are being built into a spiritual house [residence] for a holy priesthood, to offer spiritual sacrifices that are acceptable to God through Jesus Christ.

Hebrews 3:5 but Christ was faithful as a Son over His house [dwelling place]—whose house [dwelling place] we are, if we hold firmly to our confidence and the boast of our hope.

Ephesians 2:21—22 in whom the whole building, being fitted together, is growing into a holy temple in the Lord, [22]in whom you also are being built together into a dwelling of God in the Spirit.

*feel sorrowful or to promise never to repeat a sin."* It does not mean to turn and walk another way. It should mean that you end up walking another way because you have first changed your mind. Romans 12:2, which instructs us to "be transformed by the renewing of your mind," expresses the same concept as "repent." Renewing means "a renewal, renovation, complete change for the better." When our mind is changed and renewed, our actions are different. But the process of change begins with how we think and what we think. A key aspect of repentance is that it invites us to think differently about God, His heart, the Gospel, and God's view of us.

## DIFFERENTIATING BETWEEN SIN AND SINS

In the New Testament, the Greek word "hamartia," which is translated sin, is used in two different contexts. One example is Mark 2:5: "And Jesus, seeing their faith, said to the paralyzed man, 'Son, your sins are forgiven.'" This refers to missing the mark and our common understanding of sin. The second example is 2 Corinthians 15:56 "The sting of death is sin, and the power of sin is the Law." The first refers to acts or omissions; the second refers to a power system, the power of sin. Regarding the power of sin, Andrew Rillera explains how Paul described the power of sin in Romans "as a personified power and agent that deceives, enslaves, and kills and so needs to be conquered, subdued and condemned."[7] The same Greek word is used for both of these applications. The Gospel provides a remedy for both sins and the power system of sin. Not only does the Gospel provide forgiveness for sins committed, but the Gospel also provides victory over the power of sin. The Good News provides forgiveness for sins, and the Good News breaks the power of sin. The highest living is not to continue to sin because your sins have been or will be forgiven; the highest living is to break the power system of sin so that you are victorious over temptations to sin. This is the prophetic announcement that John the Baptist spoke about Jesus in John 1:29 when Jesus

---

7. Rillera, *Lamb of the Free*, 271.

came to John. "'Behold, the Lamb of God who takes away the sin of the world!'" John was declaring that Jesus was going to break the power of sin in the world, which was a different and more comprehensive provision than only forgiving sins. Because there are not two different Greek words, one must look to the context of the Scripture and the entirety of the Gospel to determine which application of "hamartia" is intended.

"Hamartia" defines sin as "to miss the mark" or "to fail at the standard," but it does not explain the origin of sin. I think it is important to endeavor to explain the origin. Eve committed humanity's first sin ever. Before she ate of the forbidden fruit of the tree of knowledge of good and evil, she had never sinned before, and she had always trusted and believed what God told her. She did not have a sin nature because she was sinless. But being sinless, she was still susceptible to believing a lie. In the garden, Eve questioned what God had said and determined that just maybe she could not trust God. From my understanding, when we sin, the root cause is that we do not trust what God has said, whether from Scripture or a specific word to us. Paul explains the same origin of sin in Romans 14:23 "But the one who doubts is condemned if he eats, because his eating is not from faith; and *whatever is not from faith is sin.*" We know that eating food is neither moral nor immoral; it is neither right nor wrong in concept. Peter's vision of the great sheet coming down with all kinds of four-footed animals and crawling creatures of the earth and birds that God declares clean confirms that eating could not be intrinsically sinful. But eating can become sin when the motivation is not trusting God. Likewise, not eating (refraining from eating or even fasting) can become sin when the motivation is fear. This is an important concept to understand. This means that our efforts to please God that originate from fear, rather than from faith (i.e., trust), actually reflect a lack of trust in God and the Scripture calls this sin. Do you realize that if tithing, Bible reading, church attendance, serving, fasting, or evangelism is done from a motivation of fear, rather than a motivation of trust or faith, that Scripture calls those activities sin?

# Chapter 4

## Impediments to Understanding the Full Message of the Gospel
*Earning or Performing*

When we believe we are worthless, without value, too broken, insignificant, or a disappointment to God, we will either work harder at earning His approval or give up trying to please God entirely. Both are destructive; both lead to hopelessness. If you are pretty good at performing, like I was, the natural course is to throw everything into serving God in order to earn His approval and affection. I spent almost 60 years in this destructive pattern of doing more and more to earn approval from both God and men. I tithed faithfully beginning as a teenager, I have read the Bible through probably 20 times, have read the New Testament probably 40 times, and I have had a morning prayer time of at least an hour for over 30 years. I fasted regularly when in law school. I would have been the model Christian except for the fact that I was trusting in my efforts to earn rather than God's work.

Discipline is very effective in changing your body. Exercise and a change of diet will affect how your body looks. Discipline will also serve to protect you. However, discipline will not change your heart; revelation changes your heart, and ultimately, being loved well and unconditionally changes your heart radically. Concentrating on spiritual disciplines is not a bad thing, but it is just the means to the end, which is to know God and come to a place of agreeing with God about your worth and value and His Love and goodness.

Personally speaking, I was a very disciplined person for years, but it never changed my heart. All my life, I had worked hard for the Lord to try to earn love and acceptance. The model that I perceived that my dad showed me was that love is earned from hard work. So I have worked hard to get God's love and approval, and worked hard to earn friends. But beginning in 2020, by God's grace and insight, God began to show me that performing well for approval and acceptance was not representative of the Kingdom of God and that it especially was not representative of God's heart. I began to experience change and insight and responded to God's invitation. I attended a men's weekend in October 2021. One of the exercises created an opportunity for God to write me a letter. It was a masterful way of hearing God without being pressured "to hear God." This is what I wrote that God wanted me to know. "I am so proud of you, my son. You are finally living like a true son, which you have always been. I am delighted by the reality that you are receiving from Me rather than trying to earn My love and acceptance. You have moved from the fields of labor to eating at My table. You are becoming a son in experience." It was perhaps the most profound thing that had ever occurred to me. God was gently adjusting how I approached and interacted with Him. As I walked away from that men's weekend, I heard God speak another truth to my heart, "Your best self is lived out of receiving from Me [God] rather than earning."

My heart was changed. Revelation of God's heart (and specifically of His incredible, unconditional, unchanging Love) for me changed my heart.[1] For years, I was convinced that I was created

---

1. "Ultimately, we will discover that study and church attendance are but forms which have little satisfaction in and of themselves. These activities must become what the Lord has ordained them to be: means through which we seek and find God. Our pleasure will be found not in the mechanics of spiritual disciplines, but that these disciplines bring us closer to God.

## IMPEDIMENTS TO UNDERSTANDING: EARNING OR PERFORMING

to serve God, and I wrongly perceived that the better I served, the more He loved me. And because I was good at serving and earning, I was proud and critical and judgmental of those who did not serve as well and or faithfully as me. However, in our relationship with God, it is not what we can give to Him or do for Him; it is about how much we receive from Him and how much we will let Him do for us. We may talk about the Gospel of grace, but too often we default to doing something for God to earn His approval or love. Sometimes it is even to pay for our failures or shortcomings. However, this is not grace, and it is not God's plan. Jesus said, "For even the Son of Man did not come to be served, but to serve, and to give His life as a ransom for many" (Mark 10:45). Ask the Lord to show you where you are trying to earn what He wants you to receive from Him freely.

What actually hinders our fellowship with the Father? What is hindering your fellowship with the Father? Before you answer my question, consider Luke 15:28–29:

> But he [the elder brother of the Prodigal Son] became angry and was not willing to go in [and eat with his father]; and his father came out and began pleading with him. ²⁹But he answered and said to his father, "Look! For so many years I have been serving you and I have never neglected a command of yours; and yet you never gave me a young goat, so that I might celebrate with my friends."

I find it very interesting that the older brother's work for his father, that his commitment to winning the father's approval and acceptance, that his diligence to "never neglect a command," that him remaining in the fields working for the Father (but away from

---

"Paul's cry was, 'That I may know Him!' (Philippians 3) It was this desire to know Jesus that produced Paul's knowledge of salvation, church order, evangelism and end time events. Out of his heart's passion to know God came revelation, the writing of Scriptures and knowledge of the Eternal. Paul's knowledge was based upon his experience with Christ. On the other hand, we have contented ourselves not with seeking the face of God, but with the facts of God. We are satisfied with a religion about Christ without the reality of Christ," (Frangipane, *The Place of Immunity*, 67.)

the Father) rather than going in and eating with his father, had a more detrimental effect on his relationship with the father than the prodigal son's sins of dishonoring his father, rebelling against his father's authority, and engaging in sinful acts. Do you see the repercussions of trying to earn approval and acceptance rather than receiving it? Notwithstanding the elder brother's refusal to celebrate with the Father and the elder brother's refusal to be with the Father, I want to focus your attention on the Father's response to the elder brother. "And he said to him, "Son, you have always been with me, and all that is mine is yours"'" (Luke 15:31). The elder son lived with a misperception of his father's love for him and therefore continued working to try to earn what he already had.

Dallas Willard is famous for a powerful statement that "Grace is not opposed to effort; it is opposed to earning."[2] Another way to say it is that our efforts to earn God's Love, approval, acceptance, and affection oppose His grace. Unfortunately, we rarely recognize it. We keep on working to earn, and when necessary, we redouble our efforts, or we finally give up entirely. An earning mentality, which I define as a practice in which you have to earn in order to receive from God, is actually an attempt to create a business transaction with God. An earning mentality greatly hinders receiving or understanding God's Love and affection because an earning mentality assumes that you have to pay a price to receive God's Love, acceptance, value, or worth. But God is not in the business of orchestrating business deals. The Gospel is not a business transaction. It is a unilateral act for which no payment or earnings are required.

Have you ever wondered why God remains faithful to His promises to us even when we are unfaithful? Because it is His unilateral act. God did not make a covenant *with us*, rather, He made a covenant (with Himself) *for us*, for our benefit. Hebrews 6:13 "For when God made the promise to Abraham, since He could swear an oath by no one greater, He swore by Himself." To use contract terms (which draws from my profession and career), God's covenant is not a contract between God and us where each party has

---

2. Willard, *The Great Omission*, 61.

to perform in order for the contract to be fulfilled; it is a contract between God and God, and we are the intended third-party beneficiaries. And God is always faithful to His promises. Therefore, if we are unfaithful, He is still faithful to the covenant because it is not transactional with us. Our inability or unwillingness to "perform" does not give rise to a breach of the covenant or a breach of contract. 2 Timothy 2:13 "If we are faithless, He remains faithful, for He cannot deny Himself." Romans 3:3 "What then? If some did not believe, their unbelief will not nullify the faithfulness of God, will it?" Did you catch it? Our unbelief does not nullify or cancel His faithfulness. Are you seeing threads of the Good News here?

Nevertheless, it is common to hear Christians say that they do not deserve to receive anything good from God. Have you ever asked God if He believes you do not deserve to receive anything good from Him? What kind of father would say that his children do not deserve anything? What kind of father would say to his children, "As your father, I owe you nothing?" Certainly, not a good father and not a loving father. Just as litmus paper indicates acid or base, this statement indicates a belief system that equates "deserving" to "earning" or "performing." If deserving is the same as having earned, then the statement would be true, because in that scenario we would have to earn in order to deserve.

But isn't deserving of God based upon relationship and love? Our children deserve certain things from their parents even when they are not earned. I think it is the same with God; we deserve not because we earn, but because of His Love relationship with us. But as long as we hold to an earning mentality, as long as we feel we deserve nothing from God or that we are insignificant, we have misunderstood God's heart, and we will overlay our earning mentality over His promises.

As a child of a loving Father, you deserve it because you are His child, created by Him in His likeness and image. Jesus clearly established this principle in the parable of the prodigal son. When the younger son returned from his independence and rebellion, he concluded that he was not worthy to be a son; he hoped he could simply live as a servant. The younger son wrongly believed that he was not worthy to be a son (Luke 15:19) based on his performance and failures. However, the father in the parable corrects the younger son's false belief system by affirming that the younger son was indeed worthy to be a son, not based upon his performance or actions, but based upon relationship and Love.

All of us want to be significant or have significance, which could be described as having worth and being recognized as important and valuable to others. Significance, worth, and value are closely related. But if you are working to become significant or valuable, you will erroneously perceive the Gospel as an obligation rather than an invitation, and this obligation to become significant or valuable will *weigh you down and wear you out*. Realizing that you are, and that you have always been, significant, valuable, worthy, and loved by God empowers you to cease trying to earn. You have always been significant! Your greatest significance comes from the fact that God created you in His image and likeness, and that He loves you with His amazing, magnificent, unconditional, unwavering, unearned, never-ending Love. When you believe and receive that God loves you completely and unconditionally and that you are significant, worthy, and valuable, that beautiful understanding enables you to stop trying to earn and leads to your greatest joy as you live from your security in His Love and affection. I have lived both ways, and living from the latter—from receiving rather than earning—is life-giving and joyful.

# Chapter 5

## What Has God Done for Us?

SIMPLY STATED, THE GOOD News of the Gospel is about what God has done for us. Therefore, we turn to the question, "What has God done for us? What has God done for humanity? What has God done for you?" The simple answer to this question is that God did everything for us. Peter expresses this concept as follows "For His divine power has granted to us everything pertaining to life and godliness, through the true knowledge of Him who called us [to] His own glory and excellence" (2 Peter 1:3). I have read this verse's amazing promise for years, but I have had a hard time connecting my life to the promise. I want to break down the various components of what God has accomplished for us because it is the Good News. God's work is not linear and is more interconnected and integrated than outlined below, but I will attempt to address each provision in a semi-segregated fashion.

But before moving to specific aspects of God's provisions, let's look at some general descriptions of God's work and God's intention for us. God "qualifies us to share in the inheritance of the saints in light" (Colossians 1:12). His intention and plan is "to present you before Him holy and blameless and beyond reproach"

(Colossians 1:22) and to "present *every person* complete in Christ" (Colossians 1:28). This plan looks impossible to us. Still, God intends to fully and completely accomplish it. In fact, God already accomplished it in you (no matter who you are) and therefore, you are holy, blameless, beyond reproach, and complete in Christ. As the Lord declared through Isaiah, "Declaring the end from the beginning, and from ancient times things which have not been done, Saying, 'My plan will be established, And I will accomplish all My good pleasure.'"

Therefore, the simple reason that these things are true for you is not because of your work or effort to earn, but because of the Godhead's decision and Christ's work, which are completed. Let's go back to the richness of Colossians to confirm the fulfillment of the promise. Colossians 2:10 "[A]nd in Him you have been made complete, and He is the head over every ruler and authority." Notice the tense of the verb; not that "you will be made complete," but that "you have been made complete." It is a done deal, a finished work. The Gospel is such Good News that your only task is to believe it and begin to live according to who God says you already are!

Paul paints this same picture in Galatians 4 when he compares the life of the heir and the slave. The heir was always an heir. There was never a time when the heir was not the heir. But there was a time when the heir lived like a slave, even though he was not a slave and even though he was the heir. This is the perfect picture of the Good News. You are a son or daughter of God, have always been a son or daughter of God, will always be a son or daughter of God, but like me and everyone else, there are times when you live like a slave rather than like an heir. There may have even been times when you declared that you do not want to be an heir, and you may have rejected being the heir. You may have tried to disown the Father and leave the family. You may have threatened to become emancipated from God. But these actions and beliefs never changed the fact that you are a child, an heir.

While Paul uses the metaphor of an heir, Peter uses the metaphor of an alien versus having been chosen and accepted. "Peter, an apostle of Jesus Christ, To those who reside as aliens, scattered throughout Pontus, Galatia, Cappadocia, Asia, and Bithynia, who are chosen" (1 Peter 1:1, NASB95). Peter is contrasting that, notwithstanding that a person has been chosen, you can still live as an alien and believe that your identity is an alien. From both of these Scriptures, we see that you are complete in Christ, but there are times (and sometimes long seasons) when you do not live like you are complete. You are chosen, holy, blameless, and beyond reproach, but sometimes it seems too unbelievable to really embrace. So we live inconsistent with who God says we are. The Gospel is the message of who you are according to God; that you are the heir and have always been; that you are chosen and have always been. And sometimes it seems too good to be true!

In answering the question "What Has God Done for Us?" specifically, we will address the following: God Forgave Us, God Included Us in Christ, God Broke the Power of Sin and Death over Us, and God Caused Us to be Born Again.

# Chapter 6

# God Forgave All Our Sins

THE GOOD NEWS BEGINS with a declaration that no matter who you are, no matter what you believe, no matter where you live, no matter if you have ever called out to God, no matter what religion you follow, God has forgiven your sins. I understand that this is probably different from what you have been taught and how you have lived, but let's see what Scripture has to say about God's forgiveness.

We will begin this topic of God's forgiveness with 2 Corinthians 5:19: "Namely, that God was in Christ reconciling the world to Himself, not counting their wrongdoings against them, and He has committed to us the word of reconciliation." Paul tells us that God was not counting our wrongdoings or our sins against us. And when does this occur? Not when we pray a prayer; not when we come forward; not when we are baptized. It happened during the crucifixion. That's Good News, isn't it! And Paul goes further to say that we are to proclaim the word that we have been reconciled, not proclaim a method or process to become reconciled.

Notice the difference between saying that something is already done and accomplished, as compared to saying that it is yet to be done. However, it seems that our approach (that my approach in the past) has been to tell people that "God *was counting* their wrongdoings and sins against them," but that if they would follow the right process and go through the right steps—which is different from group to group and denomination to denomination—that God would no longer count their sins against them. But the flip side is that if they do not "repent" with the right method, the right prayer, the right baptism, and at the right time, then God will continue counting their sins against them.

Certainly, there is an aspect of the preceding two sentences that actually is not Good News. However, if God was not and is not counting our sins against us—if 2 Corinthians 5:19 is true—then our methods to lead people to Christ are not aligning with the Scripture. Here is the question to contemplate: Are we telling unbelievers that God is "counting their wrongdoings against them" in order to persuade them to make a decision to accept Christ? Is our method actually misrepresenting the Father's heart and Jesus's completed work on the cross? Does it even sound like Good News to the unbelievers if we tell them that God is counting their sins against them? Isn't that bad news?

Perhaps we should share the even better news that God is *not* counting our sins against us. Try sharing this with the unbeliever, the atheist, the Jew, the Muslim, and the Hindu. The same God who loved us before we ever loved Him also forgave us and reconciled us before we ever asked to be reconciled. This is indeed Good News for everyone. Also, we could follow the example of the apostles in Acts and proclaim to them that Jesus has forgiven their sins. Acts 13:38 "Therefore let it be known to you, brothers, that through Him forgiveness of sins is proclaimed to you." I know that this creates other questions, that may make us uncomfortable and that we do not want to contemplate, but I trust God will continue to reveal, correct, and clarify the Good News of the Gospel. Colossians 2:13 also tells us that our sins were forgiven so that we could be made alive. "And when you were dead in your wrongdoings and the uncircumcision of your flesh, He made you alive together with Him, *having forgiven us all our wrongdoings.*" Who did He forgive?

All of us. If He forgave us our sins while we were still dead, did He not do the same with the unbeliever, the atheist, the Jew, the Muslim, and the Hindu? Rather than approaching a non-believer with the threat of hell and judgment, introduce them to the good, kind, and loving God who chose to forgive them even when they were still dead in unbelief.

Recently, as I was contemplating this provision, I was challenged to read Acts again with a view to what message the apostles proclaimed and whether the apostles' messages were consistent or inconsistent with the above points. I will share a bit of what I found. First, the word "hell" does not appear in Acts, nor in any of the books written by Paul. Punishment does not appear in Acts, and fire only appears as a physical reaction as a source of heat. There are 25 instances where Acts records what the apostles declared or preached. (See Appendix A for a listing of each of these verses.) Many of the instances describe the message as being about the Kingdom of God, which itself is instructive of its priority. However, not in one single instance did the Apostles instruct the people to pray a prayer or comply with a certain process in order to be forgiven. The clearest passage of the proclaimed message is Acts 13:38-39 "Therefore let it be known to you, brothers, that *through Him forgiveness of sins is proclaimed* to you, ³⁹and through Him everyone who believes is freed from all things, from which you could not be freed through the Law of Moses." This is the same message as 2 Corinthians 5:19 (that God was reconciling the world to himself in Christ, not counting people's sins against them). The apostles did not give the people a process for getting their sins forgiven; they proclaimed that their sins were forgiven, in stark contrast to our modern, well-intentioned approach.

Where did the apostles get this? Where did they hear it? From Acts 4:20, we understand the principle that the apostles only repeated what they had seen and what they had heard. Had the apostles heard Jesus proclaiming the forgiveness of sins rather than a process or procedure to follow in order to be forgiven? The Old Covenant had an elaborate process by which sins were pushed forward (not forgiven) and people and utensils were cleansed. Would

Jesus offer another process? After the resurrection, Jesus appeared to the disciples, and his interaction is recorded in Luke 24. From verses 45–47, we see the same approach to forgiveness of sins. "Then He opened their minds to understand the Scriptures, [46]and He said to them, 'So it is written, that the Christ would suffer and rise from the dead on the third day, [47]and that *repentance for forgiveness of sins would be proclaimed in His name* to all the nations, beginning from Jerusalem.'" In Luke 24 we have Jesus proclaiming that there would be a "change of thinking" regarding forgiveness. Forgiveness would no longer be a prescribed process to be repeated over and over. Forgiveness of sins would now be proclaimed. The apostles repeat that proclamation throughout Acts.

When Paul makes his defense before King Agrippa in Acts 26, he recounts the conversation that he received from the Lord on his way to Damascus.

> "[16]But get up and stand on your feet; for this purpose I have appeared to you, to appoint you as a servant and a witness not only to the things in which you have seen Me, but also to the things in which I will appear to you, [17]rescuing you from the Jewish people and from the Gentiles, to whom I am sending you, [18]*to open their eyes so that they may turn from darkness to light,* and from *the power of Satan to God*, that they *may receive forgiveness of sins* and an inheritance among those who have been sanctified by faith in Me."

Just like the apostles who walked with Jesus and followed His example in proclaiming forgiveness of sins, Jesus appeared to Paul, giving him instruction regarding his calling and his message. The instructions were directly from Jesus, and Jesus did not give Paul a process or formula. Jesus did not suggest an improved sacrificial system. There were no creeds to recite nor any actions to take. Just as we have seen with the message proclaimed by the apostles earlier, Paul's purpose was to work with God so that the eyes of the Gentiles may be opened in order that they would believe Paul's proclamation of the Gospel that God had forgiven the Gentiles' sins. Paul's function was to announce that their sins had been forgiven and encourage them to receive this incredible gift.

Does this really mean that our sins are forgiven without the necessity of praying the "sinner's prayer?" Is it possible to be forgiven without praying a prayer? Perhaps it is best to look at Jesus's situations where He "forgave sin." There are only two recorded instances where Jesus proclaims that a person's sins are forgiven. In Matthew 9:2, friends of a paralyzed man brought the friend to Jesus on a stretcher. "And seeing their faith, Jesus said to the man who was paralyzed, 'Take courage, son; your sins are forgiven.'" (See also Mark 2:5 and Luke 5:20). Do you find that the paralyzed man prayed a prayer? Did he even ask to be forgiven?

The other instance where Jesus "forgave sin" is found in Luke 7:36–50 where a woman in the city who was a sinner; brought an alabaster vial of perfume, stood behind Him at His feet, weeping, wet His feet with her tears, wiped them with the hair of her head, and began kissing His feet and anointing them with the perfume. After the Pharisee's indignant response, Jesus said to her, "Your sins have been forgiven" (Luke 7:48). Notice the past tense of the verb. Did the woman of the city pray a prayer or ask to be forgiven? You can't find any evidence of that.

Let's also look at another Old Testament example based upon the fact that Jesus is our intercessor. For a picture of the impact of an intercessor, we can look to Moses, who intercedes for the Israelites before the Lord as recorded in Numbers 14. There were estimated to be 3 million Israelites at this time, none of whom are said to have been repentant or to have confessed their sins. We have no evidence that any of them had a broken, contrite spirit. Still, Moses intercedes for them in Numbers 14:19: "Please forgive the guilt of this people in accordance with the greatness of Your mercy, just as You also have forgiven this people, from Egypt even until now." And look to Verse 20 for the Lord's response, "So the LORD said, 'I have forgiven them in accordance with your word.'" Wow, the Lord confirms that He has forgiven 3 million Israelites who are not repentant because Moses intercedes. It is also important to note that Moses did not offer any sacrifice in order for God to forgive their sins, but more on the lack of sacrifice later.

Do you think Moses is a more effective intercessor than Jesus? Moses prays 28 words, and three million Israelites are forgiven and saved from the plague and death. For whom do you think Jesus is interceding? Do you know that Jesus is interceding for you? On the cross, Jesus says, "Forgive them, Father."[1] Even if at that time Jesus limited that prayer of forgiveness to his executioners, we know from John 3:16 that He came for the whole world. And we also know that "He always lives to make intercession for [us]." Can we see from Moses how quickly the Father is to forgive and pardon? His heart is to forgive; that is what Love does. The Lord forgave the Israelites according to Moses's word. And He will do the same according to Jesus's Word because Jesus's words were in agreement with God's heart. Jesus did not have to convince the Father. He did not even have to be asked, because forgiving even without being asked is consistent with Love. Jesus prayed the very word He heard the Father speak, which was forgiveness. Jesus is interceding for you (no matter who you are or what you have done or what you think about Him). And He is praying a more complete and transformative prayer than Moses prayed, for you. Oh, what a complete Savior! If it is this clear, then why have we not known this before? Because we have been conditioned to read the Scripture to say and mean what we have been told it is supposed to say and mean.

I will directly say to you, "Your sins are forgiven." No matter who you are or what you have done. No matter whether you are ready to live as a forgiven person, your sins are still forgiven. God made a decision before time, but implemented during the crucifixion, to forgive your sins. If you do not believe it, He still forgave

---

1. Luke 23:34 But Jesus was saying, "Father, forgive them; for they do not know what they are doing." When considering this verse, we must remember that Jesus said multiply times that He only said and only did what He heard and saw the Father doing. When Jesus makes the statement "forgive them Father," He is agreeing with the Father's deep longing and desire for mankind. Jesus is not intervening to try to change the Father's heart from wrathful anger to forgiveness; He is agreeing with the Father's kind, generous, loving, forgiving heart.

your sins. If you don't want it, He still forgave your sins. It is by His decision and His grace. Some of you will rightfully ask what happens if you do not accept to receive God's forgiveness. The clearest answer is that you will live as if you are unforgiven; you will live as if you are separated from God. Although we are focused on forgiveness (being justified), we can take an important concept from Paul's statement about salvation found in Ephesians 2:8 "For by grace you have been saved through faith; and this [salvation] is not of yourselves, it is the gift of God."

The evidence of God's decision to forgive our sins is everywhere, but our traditional understanding of salvation hinders us from seeing this incredible provision. We read *quid pro quo* into the Scripture. We have been taught over and over that God was angry at man because man sinned, and that God had to have a punching bag upon whom to release His anger. Jesus was the punching bag, and now God is satisfied enough that He forgives us. This approach disregards that forgiveness is a product of God's Love for us, but rather promotes that forgiveness is a result of an intervention by Jesus, which strips God's Love from the process. And then we are left to submit and follow, and love a God who is angry.

But this whole *quid pro quo* approach to forgiveness described above is transactional, requiring a payment in order to receive forgiveness. Forgiveness, however, is a loving decision, not a contract. The transactional approach radically misrepresents God. In Hebrews 8, the writer of Hebrews quotes from Jeremiah in declaring the fulfillment of Jeremiah's prophetic message about a New Covenant with the house of Israel and the house of Judah. The new covenant includes a grace-filled approach to sins, as contrasted with the sacrificial system of the Levitical law, as we see in verse 12. "FOR I WILL BE MERCIFUL TOWARD THEIR WRONGDOINGS, AND THEIR SINS I WILL NO LONGER REMEMBER." It confirms that forgiveness of sins is not a transactional undertaking, but rather that it is a unilateral decision of a loving and kind God. In the New Covenant, which Jeremiah foresaw and which God proclaimed, forgiveness of sins would no longer be conditional or dependent upon the offering of sacrifices.

God chooses and elects to forgive sin based solely upon His mercy and His nature of Love.

For as much as the above Scriptures seem to indicate that God decided to forgive us, how can we get around the other verses that seem to indicate that it requires our faith and our belief; how can we get around the other verses that seem to indicate that forgiveness is not a unilateral action; how can we get around the necessity of praying the sinner's prayer? These questions were where I struggled the most in attempting to reconcile Scriptures that seemed contradictory. The question I wrestled with was whether I had to believe or have faith in order to become justified? Stated another way, the question I wrestled with was whether I had to believe or have faith in order for my sins to be forgiven? Justification certainly requires faith, but it is not our faith that justifies us, it is Christ's faith. Let's explore this topic and look at a few verses about which you are probably saying, *"but what about . . . ."*

Let's begin with Romans 4:5: "But to the one who does not work, but believes *in Him who justifies* the ungodly, his faith is *reckoned* as righteousness." Looking at this verse and similar verses,[2] there are two verbs: justified and reckoned. They are not synonymous, but I have treated them as synonymous my entire life. Treating them as synonymous, when they are different has resulted in my confusion. Justify means "to render or make one righteous or just." Reckon means "to figure out, to conclude, to count, to compute, to determine, to analyze." To justify—what God does—is to make us righteous. It is the action; it affects a change; it changes our status substantively; it is creative. God justifies the ungodly. The Greek word translated as "to reckon" is also an accounting term. In business, accounting departments and accounting functions do not create profits or sales; they account for profits that have already been earned. To reckon is not creative; it does not change our status; it makes us aware of our already existing status.

---

2. Romans 4:3 "For what does the Scripture say? 'Abraham believed God and it was credited to him as righteousness.'" Credited to is the same Greek word translated as "reckoned" in Romans 4:5. Also, the same Greek word is translated as "credited to" in Galatians 3:6 and James 2:23.

To reckon is to figure out that which is already true; that He has made me righteous by forgiving my sins, as explained in 2 Corinthians 5:19. Another way to describe this verse is that "to reckon" means to become aware of what is already true. Once I believe that it is already true, then, like Abraham, I cease from works to create my righteousness; I trust His act of having justified me.

Then what part do we have in *being justified?* None! This is entirely covered in God's decision and by God's provision. I know this challenges what you have been taught and what you have believed. Remember, redemption is a *divine provision*, and justification is a *divine pronouncement or a divine change of status*. And now we come to an important truth: that we do not always live according to God's truth about who we are. Therefore, I can be forgiven and justified freely, but not believe it, not receive it, and/or not accept it. Then what part do I have in *living justified?* I will have to believe God by reckoning (concluding, determining, becoming aware, believing) so that I live according to what God has already done for me and declared about me. Reckoning does not make me righteous; it enables me to see that God had already made and declared me righteous. What if I do not believe? I am still justified, but I will not experience the blessedness of that assurance. If I do not reckon, I will be like the heir in Galatians 4:1 who subjectively lives like a slave although objectively he is the owner of everything. Reckoning enables you to live as God has declared you to be. Reckoning refutes the lies that say that you are not worthy, that you are not enough, or that you must do more. It refutes the lies like: "You should have prayed in a different way," "You should have been baptized differently," and "You should have done more."

But Romans 4:5 is just one verse, and you are still probably saying, "but what about . . . ." So let's go to a series of verses that all have similar translation errors.

Galatians 2:16 "[N]evertheless, knowing that a person is not justified by works of the Law but through faith *in* Christ Jesus, even we have believed in Christ Jesus, so that we may be justified by faith *in* Christ and not by works of the Law; since by works of the Law no flesh will be justified." Notwithstanding what Romans

4:5 says, Galatians 2:16 seems clear that we are justified by faith. And we are indeed justified by faith, but it is Christ's faith, not our faith. The preposition "*in*" which is italicized above in two (2) places has been added by the translators. There are a couple of Greek words for "in" and neither of them are found in the original Greek. The case of the noun Christ is genitive (possessive), translated in English as Christ's (that is, of Christ, belonging to Christ, etc.). It should read literally and correctly ". . . but through Christ Jesus's faith, even we have believed in Christ Jesus so that we may be justified by Christ's faith and not by works of the Law." This is easily verified by using Blue Letter Bible or other Bible resources that give the Greek word in the original for every translated word. The translators also changed the meaning of Romans 3:22 by adding the word "*in*." "But it is the righteousness of God through faith *in* Jesus Christ for all those who believe; for there is no distinction." The preposition "*in*" is likewise not in the original Greek, and the verse should read, "but righteousness of God through Jesus Christ's faith for all those who believe."

This addition of extra words by the translators is repeated in Galatians 2:20, Galatians 3:2, Galatians 3:5, and Philippians 3:9. Galatians 2:20 "I have been crucified with Christ; and it is no longer I who live, but Christ lives in me; and the life which I now live in the flesh I live by faith *in* the Son of God, who loved me and gave Himself up for me." In Galatians 2:20, as in Galatians 2:16, there is no preposition between faith and the Son of God. Grammatically, and in its genitive case, it should read, "I live by the Son of God's faith, who loved me and gave Himself up for me." Let's also look at Galatians 3:2 and 3:5: "This is the only thing I want to find out from you: did you receive the Spirit by works of the Law, or by hearing *with* faith?" Galatians 3:5 "So then, does He who provides you with the Spirit and works miracles among you, do it by works of the Law, or by hearing *with* faith?" In both Galatians 3:2 and 3:5, there is no preposition between hearing and faith in the Greek. The preposition "*with*" has also been added by the translators. The addition implies that hearing had to combine with our faith, but the hearing is about faith, about Christ's faith, that He believed for us because, in our weakness and vulnerability, we were incapable of believing.

Lastly, let's consider Philippians 3:9: "and may be found in Him, not having a righteousness of my own derived from the Law, but that which is through faith *in* Christ, the righteousness which comes from God on the basis of faith." In Philippians 3:9, there is no preposition between faith and Christ in the Greek manuscripts. The preposition "*in*" was likewise added by the translators. The NASB has a footnote that the word "in" could be "through the faithfulness of Christ," which is the correct translation. Looking further in Philippians 3:9, the verse even confirms it "comes from God."

Now let's look at one last verse where the translators added a word. Romans 10:10 "for with the heart man believes resulting in righteousness . . . ." "Resulting" is not in the Greek as the translators added it as well. The word "in" which means "into, unto, to, towards, for, among," is inaccurately translated as "resulting in." "*In*" is a preposition, but translated as a form of a verb. The Greek word "in" is found 1,744 times in the New Testament, and I have not found any other time when it is translated in the form of a verb rather than a preposition. It should read, "for with the heart man believes in righteousness." We believe that Christ has made us righteous by His completed work. Translated correctly, it once again moves the story from my effort to God's provision, and therefore to believing what God has already done.

This may be a lot to process, but fortunately, we have the original Greek wording from which you can easily determine when words have been added. The added words change the intent substantially. But how would I harmonize Romans 5:1: "Therefore, having been justified by faith, we have peace with God through our Lord Jesus Christ"? No words were added to this verse. As I was contemplating this verse, I realized something had been added—punctuation. There was no punctuation in the original Greek. Translators added it where they thought it was best to add, and the comma placement makes a huge difference. When asking the Lord about this verse, I had a quiet impression, "Move the comma because men inserted the punctuation." And here is the result of moving the comma: "Therefore, having been justified, by faith we have peace with God through our Lord Jesus Christ." As I said, comma placement makes a huge difference. It takes our faith (our believing) to accept the peace we have with God, but it does not require our faith to be justified.

Any singular verse taken out of the context of the larger and entire plan of God, but without aligning it to God's heart of Love, can confuse us. Also, some verses simply do not seem to align nicely with other verses. I know it is an impossible task to remove all ambiguity or apparent conflict, and that is not my stated goal. An example of a verse which would seem to contradict the foregoing discussion about forgiveness is Ephesians 1:7: "In Him we have redemption through His blood, the forgiveness of our wrongdoings, according to the riches of His grace." The Greek word for wrongdoings is not "hamartia," the word which is used for sin or sins as explained above. In Ephesians 1:7, we read it as sins, and most translations interpret it as sins because we have been taught to think that the Gospel is primarily, if not exclusively, about having our sins forgiven so that we can go to heaven when we die.

When we realize that the Gospel is not primarily about forgiveness of sin and avoiding hell, there is freedom to search out the intention in light of God's heart and comprehensive plan. The Greek word translated as wrongdoings is actually "paraptōma," which Strong defines as "to fall beside or near something, or a lapse or deviation from truth and uprightness." Further, when you look at the Greek word translated as "forgiveness," Strong's first definition is to "release from bondage or imprisonment." Using these two definitions means that a very valid translation of the verse would be, "In Him we have redemption through His blood, the release from bondage or imprisonment from our wrong thinking and our belief in untruth, according to the riches of His grace." That interpretation would fit hand in glove with my points in this chapter. But even if some verses appear to remain incongruent with other verses (which I freely acknowledge), such apparent inconsistency does not shake my belief in the whole of the Good News.

Now let us turn to the story of the servant whose debt was forgiven by the king (Matthew 18:21–35), but who had his own debtor thrown in prison. He never asked that the king forgive his debt. Nevertheless, the king forgave him just as we see in 2 Corinthians 5:19, without even being asked to forgive. If nothing more can be learned from this parable, the *king's unilateral decision to forgive the debt is an amazing picture of God's grace to forgive without ever being asked.* What is the point of the parable, then? Just as we often do not think that God has forgiven us or cannot forgive us unless we do something (unless we earn our forgiveness or at least a portion of it), the issue is that the forgiven servant did not really realize that the king had forgiven his debt. The forgiven servant continued to live as if he was not forgiven. He continued to live as if he had an enormous debt to the king. I base this on his actions and response.

When he came to the king, he did not ask for the debt to be forgiven, just that the king would have patience and give him more time to pay. He even says, I will "repay you everything." In response, the king released him from the debt. That was more than he had asked for. Maybe he could not receive more than he asked for or requested, which was only the king's patience and an extension of time. Perhaps he did not receive the offered forgiveness; maybe he had only received the requested extension, which means that he focused on collecting what was due him from his debtors so that he could endeavor to repay the king. Remember, he promised to repay everything. If he had received the king's forgiveness, he would have been out celebrating. If he had received his forgiveness, there would have been no reason to collect the few dollars from his debtor in order to use it to pay the king. Perhaps he could not extend forgiveness because he never received forgiveness even though it was extended and made available to him, an example of "you cannot give what you have not first received!" (See Colossians 3:13 "bearing with one another, and forgiving each other, whoever has a complaint against anyone; just as the Lord forgave you, so you also.") You cannot forgive until you know and receive that you are forgiven.

Look at Matthew 18:34 "And his master, moved with anger, handed him over to the torturers until he would repay all that was owed him." Let us also remember that the master/king was kind and compassionate, or he would never have forgiven the huge debt in the first instance. You must interpret this in light of the king's kind and compassionate heart to forgive. So let's look for kindness and compassion, and mercy in the king's response. How much was the master owed? At this point, *the master was owed nothing;* verse 32 tells us that everything the servant had owed had been forgiven. Therefore, the servant owed nothing; he just had not yet come to understand that he had been forgiven. The master's anger was directed against the blockage or the lie that kept the servant from receiving his forgiveness of debt. It was not directed against the servant.

Therefore, being handed over to the torturers was not in order for the king to get repaid because the king had already forgiven all of the debt and was owed nothing; being handed over to the torturers was not for the servant to be punished, but for the servant to come to realize he had been fully forgiven. It was for the servant to realize that he owed nothing, a concept that he had not yet grasped; forgiveness of debt that he had yet to accept. I believe the king was angry about the lie that hindered the servant from believing that he was fully forgiven. Therefore, the king turned him over to torturers so that he might realize that he had been forgiven everything. It was a redemptive "torture." The king did not instruct him to forgive, but strategically positioned him to first receive forgiveness so that he could be forgiving of his creditors. The king knew that he would be unable to forgive others until he first realized that he had been forgiven everything. Give me the liberty to imagine the conversation in the servant's head as he is "handed over to the torturers" until he could repay.

"*I will never be able to repay this debt. It is more than I could ever make in a whole lifetime. I am doomed to be here forever. How does the king expect me to ever be able to repay this? My life is over. I have no hope at all. What was it that the king told me? Let me see if I can remember the exact words that the king said. I do remember the king said, 'I forgive your debt; it is forgiven and wiped out.' Do you think the king was serious? Will he really forgive all of my debt without me even paying a penny? That is what he said. How could I have missed it? Why was I trying to repay what the king had forgiven?"* And then he declares and proclaims forcefully and aloud to the torturers, *"Hey, there is nothing to be repaid. The debt is zero. Although I did not pay it, the king forgave the debt. I no longer owe anything. I am free of the debt."*

As I conclude this section on God's forgiveness, I know what you are thinking: "Are you saying I can sin in any way I want and get away with it?" You never get away with sin. There is always a price for sin. Sin has consequences. Romans 6:23 confirms that sin brings consequences, and the most profound consequence is death, which I will address in a subsequent chapter. All sin is based on believing a lie. Jesus tells us that the truth sets us free and gives us life. That means that believing a lie brings us bondage and steals our life. Following the words of truth is life-giving. Following a lie steals your life and joy. Sin is believing a lie rather than what God says is best for you. For example, God calls you to forgive an offender because God knows that is the best life for you. If you do not forgive and hold an offense, God forgives you of your lack of obedience as stated above, but you still suffer the consequences of your disobedience. You will carry bitterness around. You will occupy your mind contemplating how to get even. You will feel a weight. Therefore, sin carries with it its own consequences. For instance, John tells us in 1 John 3:15 that if we hate a brother or sister, *eternal life does not remain in him.* That does not mean that there is none of Christ's life in you at all, but that you cannot hold unforgiveness and God's life in the same space at the same time. *Hate or unforgiveness push out the life that God offers us daily.* As a Christian culture, we have focused almost exclusively on the belief that God imposes punishment for our sin as our singular motivation to obey God. As a result, we have missed the reason God calls us to obey Him, because it is for our very best life; it is for an abundant life every day. I repeat, God has already forgiven your sins. However, He has not eliminated the consequences of your sin.

Your sins, although forgiven, will destroy you, they will destroy your peace, they will leave you hopeless, they will harm others, they will destroy relationships. Therefore, you cannot believe and follow a lie (sin) and get away with it because the consequences of sin will affect your life and your relationships. Your behavior and your actions will affect your abundant life every day. And it will most likely affect your perception of your relationship with God, although it does not affect God's relationship with you. Because He is loving, kind, good, and never separates from us, He does not distance Himself from us even when we blatantly disobey.

I will rephrase your question. "Are you saying I can disobey God and remain secure in His Love and forgiveness?" Yes, that is exactly what I am saying! Our motivation for obeying God does not have to lie in avoiding punishment, wrath, or separation; our motivation for obeying God is that the God who loves us perfectly would only call us and invite us into opportunities that bring abundant life. Why would I want to miss invitations for abundant life? Paul had the same understanding, and he responds in a similar fashion in Romans 6:1–2: "What shall we say then? Are we to continue in sin so that grace may increase? ²Far from it! How shall we who died to sin still live in it?" Paul did not correct the Romans by saying that grace would not cover their transgressions. Paul does not warn the Romans that grace is scarce or limited or not available. Paul is reminding the Romans of who they are—new creatures in Christ who can choose life-giving decisions. This will likely raise another concern—that my understanding and application of Scripture have simply created a license to pursue our own agenda and will. My question in response is why would you look for a license to pursue your own agenda and will (which is not life-giving) once you have discovered that God absolutely loves and adores you and that He knows what brings you the most life. God's plan of redemption was never intended so that I could live independently, but that I might have an abundant life. God is not endeavoring to limit my life and joy; He wants me to receive abundant life and limitless joy.

Furthermore, let us not forget that "he saved us, not because of righteous things we had done, but because of his mercy" (Titus 3:5 (a)). Even though Paul is addressing the process of salvation rather than being justified and being made righteous, the principle that God, rather than we, accomplishes the work is applicable. If we are not saved by the righteous things we have done, then we are also not saved by abstaining from the unrighteous things. The righteous things and abstaining from the unrighteous things are the fruit of a person who, in God's great mercy, realizes that he or she is securely positioned in Christ and God's Love. And to go a step further, not performing a righteous act or performing an unrighteous act, does not change who we are—children of God who are justified by mercy with a new life in the Holy Spirit and dearly loved by God. Our identity does not change based on our behavior or our actions.

Quoting Martyn Lloyd-Jones:

> The true preaching of the Gospel of salvation by grace alone always leads to the possibility of this charge being brought against it. There is no better test as to whether a man is really preaching the New Testament Gospel of salvation than this, that some people might misunderstand it and misinterpret it to mean that it really amounts to this, that because you are saved by grace alone it does not matter at all what you do; you can go on sinning as much as you like because it will resound all the more to the glory of grace.[3]

Did you catch Martyn Lloyd-Jones's litmus test of whether the Gospel being proclaimed is the Gospel of grace? *If the message cannot be accused of being misused, then it likely isn't the full Gospel.* That is something to contemplate. The above discussion on forgiveness, however, may have left you contemplating what role salvation plays in our lives.

---

3. Lloyd-Jones, *Romans: An exposition of Chapter 6*, 8.

# Chapter 7

## God Has a Plan for Your Deliverance, Freedom, and Salvation

WHILE YOU ARE PART of humanity and a beneficiary of God's thorough and complete redemptive and transformational work for all of humanity, you are also an individual. You have experienced unique pain, rejection, abuse, and fears. Some Christian teaching and interpretations of Biblical doctrines have misrepresented God's heart to you in unique and various, but detrimental ways. These events have opened the door to misperceptions, resulting in false beliefs about yourself and God. The lies we most commonly believe are "I am not enough; I have to do more," "I am not loved," and "God will leave me or God has left me." Every lie we entertain or believe steals life from us, because our lives are designed to run on truth, just as vehicles are designed to run on gasoline or diesel. If you put gasoline fuel in a vehicle designed to run on diesel fuel, you will injure or maybe destroy the vehicle. If we are going to have an abundant life, it is necessary to live from principles of truth rather than from lies about ourselves, lies about God, and lies about others.

You will not experience deliverance, freedom, and salvation, and thus become whole, until the lies and misperceptions are replaced with truth. But never fear, God has a unique and individual plan for you to become free, healed, and whole, and this is Biblical salvation. *His* heart desires that you become free, healed, and whole, and He has a plan for you to fulfill *His* heart's desire. This explanation of salvation gives personal meaning and application to Jeremiah 29:11: "'For I know the plans that I have for you,' declares the LORD, 'plans for [salvation] and not for disaster, to give you a future and a hope.'" Personally, His plan for me included experiencing freedom from the mistaken belief that I had to perform well in order to earn God's Love. Even though I was almost 60 before I started to believe and live this truth, coming to an understanding and belief that God really does love me unconditionally was the most transformative experience of my Christian walk. Deliverance from the lie regarding God's unconditional love and freedom to trust Him rather than working to earn His Love and approval is an important aspect of how salvation looked in my life. I have been saved from my wrong beliefs, and I am being saved from my wrong beliefs.

As explained above, salvation is a process, and because it is a process, it is best understood as being past tense, present tense, and future tense. God has provided everything necessary for your salvation to be complete. Although your justification (forgiveness of sins) was a unilateral decision of God before the creation of the world, your process of salvation requires your active participation through faith and belief. It takes faith to believe that you are who God says you are, so that you can live according to who God says you are. It takes faith to reject lies that you have believed about yourself and God. Paul tells us in Romans 1:16 that believing unleashes "the power of God for salvation to everyone who believes, to the Jew first and also to the Greek." And 1 Peter 1:9 tells us that faith leads to the salvation of your soul. Although your faith is not a necessary ingredient for God to forgive your sins, your faith is required to become whole and free, as Paul describes in Ephesians 2:8. Let's explore how our faith works with regard to the process of salvation.

To answer that question, let's revisit the more accurate translation of Romans 10:9–10 now that we have established that the translators added words which changed the meaning. "That if you confess with your mouth Jesus as Lord, and believe in your heart that God raised Him from the dead, you will be saved; ¹⁰for with the heart a person believes [] in righteousness, and with the mouth he confesses, [] in salvation." "Confesses "is the Greek word "homologeō" which means "to say the same thing as another." If you look at the Greek word, you can easily see a compound word "homo" which means "same" and "logeo" which is a form of logos or the word. Your forgiveness is not dependent upon you agreeing with God; however, your salvation or sanctification is dependent upon you agreeing with God and speaking the same word that He is speaking. This requires your faith that His words to you are true. Jesus conveyed the importance of truth in John 17:17 when He asked the Father to "Sanctify them [to live in accordance with] the truth; your word is truth." God knows that if you receive and believe the truth that it will save you, sanctify you, transform you, deliver you, rescue you, and give you life. This same concept is also expressed in Romans 12:2: "And do not be conformed to this world, but be transformed by the renewing of your mind." Your life changes, and you are transformed, saved, and rescued as your way of thinking changes to align with God's way of thinking. The challenge of Christian life and Christian maturity is to believe correctly, so that you believe the truth of what God says. When you believe correctly, you end up making different decisions, life-giving decisions, and therefore you end up living differently, which is the power of truth to sanctify (John 17:17). But it begins with believing God's words of truth.

However, we are often independent and stubborn and slow to trust God's words. Still, eventually, by God's grace and patience, we will all come to realize that independence is really slavery rather than freedom. In the meantime, however, God is patient, kind, and loving as the salvation or transformation process progresses. God is not bound or limited by time; He never has been; He never will be bound or limited by time. Therefore, God is not fearful regarding time. He never analyzes from a perspective that time is going to run out or that there is not enough time. Because He is not fearful regarding time, He is patient with us in our process of salvation. "But we should always give thanks to God for you, brothers and sisters beloved by the Lord, because *God has chosen you from the beginning for salvation* through sanctification by the Spirit and faith in the truth" (2 Thessalonians 2:13). From the beginning of creation, God had already determined, planned for, and provided for your salvation. He has an individual personal plan that leads to your deliverance, freedom, and salvation. Isaiah 46:10 expresses the concept as follows: "Declaring the end from the beginning, and from ancient times things which have not been done, saying, 'My plan will be established, And I will accomplish all My good pleasure.'" You have no idea of the investment that God has in you. He has no intention of abandoning you in the process.

Paul stated it this way to the Philippians. "For I am confident of this very thing, that He who began a good work [in] you will complete it [until] the day of Christ Jesus" (Philippians 1:6). In other words, the day will not come until you have been made complete and whole. You probably want to know what I mean when I say "the day." Is it when I die, or on the judgment day, or some other marked day? I do not know when "the day" is, but we nevertheless have a promise that on "the day" you will be complete. No matter where you see yourself in relation to God, God is saving you even now, and He will continue patiently doing so. His plan is that you will become whole and complete, free of internal conflict, living in peace as you trust His words to you. "Therefore, He is also able to save [completely] those who come to God through Him, since He always lives to make intercession for them" (Hebrew 7:25).

For what is Christ interceding for us? That question is best answered by considering that there is nothing further that God needs to accomplish. Based upon 2 Peter 1:3, God has done and completed everything necessary so that we can have life and reflect His image. Based upon 2 Peter 1:3, there is nothing that we need to accomplish or perform. But we do need to receive. As Christ intercedes for us, I believe He is interceding that we would believe and receive that His divine power has granted to us everything pertaining to life and godliness. I believe He is interceding that our salvation process will be complete, that we will fully trust His promises, and that we will receive His divine power for full, abundant life and in order to display His image. I have an assurance that Christ is interceding for you until His plan for you is completed. God has saved you, He is saving you, and He will continue saving you until you receive the fullness of abundant life and display His glory. But this salvation process requires your faith to be activated to believe and trust what God speaks about you and to you. In summary, you might say that your entire Christian life is about learning to trust God's words.

# Chapter 8

## God Placed Us In Christ

IN ADDITION TO FORGIVING our sins, God placed us in Christ. "But it is [from] Him that you are in Christ Jesus, who became to us wisdom from God, and righteousness and sanctification, and redemption" (1 Corinthians 1:30). From this verse, we receive two important truths. First, God made the decision and exercised the power to place us in Christ Jesus. Second, because we are in Christ Jesus, we have been made righteousness and are being saved and sanctified. Because this is a difficult concept to comprehend, we often lay it aside or, at best, think of it allegorically only. It may even sound like a talking head because it just seems illogical to contemplate that God placed all of humanity in Christ.

I am convinced that understanding the truth that God placed you and all humanity in Christ is central to understanding the Gospel. I will go even further to venture to say that if you do not accept the truth that you have been placed in Christ (even if you do not understand it), it will be impossible for you to receive certain aspects of the Good News of the Gospel. "Being in Christ" is how the Gospel is executed in our lives; therefore, this concept deserves close attention. It works even if we do not understand it, but just a little understanding allows us to believe and receive more easily.

Several years ago, I began to see a recurring concept in Scripture. Over and over, I encountered Scripture that spoke of us as "being in Christ" and as "Christ being in us." We have been taught that Jesus came to live in our hearts (although we mostly thought of that figuratively), but trying to conceptualize how we are in Christ mostly made my head hurt. Nevertheless, I began taking notes and asking the Spirit of Truth to teach me about this concept. There are at least 46 verses that convey the concept that Christ is in us and/or that we are in Christ, and of the 46 verses, at least 26 of them convey the truth that we are in Christ. The mere number of verses began to convince me there was a fabulous truth here. When I compared this frequency to the concept of being born again, which Jesus only spoke of once (in John 3:3, 7) and Peter only spoke of once, but about which Paul never spoke at all, I was surprised.

Because the fact that you are in Christ is central to understanding the Gospel, I want to build a case and provide the Biblical evidence that "we are in Christ," by simply quoting a few of the 26 verses:

- 2 Corinthians 1:21 Now He who *establishes us with you in Christ* and anointed us is God.

- Ephesians 1:3-4 Blessed be the God and Father of our Lord Jesus Christ, who has blessed us with every spiritual blessing in the heavenly places *in Christ,* ⁴just as *He chose us in Him* before the foundation of the world, that we would be holy and blameless before Him.

- Ephesians 1:13 In Him, you also, after listening to the message of truth, the Gospel of your salvation—having also believed, you were sealed in Him with the Holy Spirit of the promise.

- Ephesians 2:10 For we are His workmanship, *created in Christ Jesus* for good works, which God prepared beforehand so that we would walk in them.

- Philippians 2:1 If you have any encouragement from being *united with Christ* (NIV).

- 1 John 4:12-13 No one has ever seen God; but if we love one another, God lives in us and his love is made complete in us. [13]This is how we know that *we live in him and he in us: He has given us of his Spirit.*

Do you see that God chose to place humanity in Christ? How are we to interpret or understand the Biblical references that we are in Christ, placed in Christ, united with Christ, or that He chose us in Him? To be in something means that you are housed or live inside it. If you are in Tennessee, that means your life and movement are occurring from a physical location in Tennessee. It is not complicated, but it can nevertheless be confusing. If we are in Christ, that simply means that our life and movement come from our placement of being inside Christ. A dear man of God and friend of mine, Alan Vincent, called this principle "the law of heredity." We see it discussed in Scripture in relation to Abraham and Levi, his great-grandson, and also in relation to Adam. Let's refresh ourselves with those verses.

In Hebrews 7, the writer is constructing an argument that the priesthood of Melchizedek is superior to the Levitical priesthood. To prove his point, he argues that the lesser (Levi) is blessed by the greater (Melchizedek), and states that Levi, who collects the tenth, actually paid the tenth to Melchizedek. But there is no record of Levi paying a tithe to Melchizedek. However, Scripture states that Abraham paid a tenth to Melchizedek. And the law of heredity is expressed as follows: "because when Melchizedek met Abraham," and paid him a tenth, "Levi was still in the body of his ancestor" (Hebrews 7:10). That which Abraham did was attributed to his great-grandson because Levi came from Abraham's body. Biblically and spiritually (as well as genetically), Levi was in Abraham. In this instance, the law of heredity worked to Levi's benefit. But the law of heredity can also be detrimental, as it was for each of us from having our heredity in Adam.

If Levi was in Abraham's body, all of humanity was in Adam's body. Romans 5:12 explains how that affected humanity, "Therefore, just as sin entered the world through one man, and death through sin, and in this way *death came to all people, because all sinned*." Each of us was subjected to the law of sin and death as a result of Adam's sin because all of humanity was in Adam. That was our inheritance from our forefather, Adam. In fact, we did not even have a choice in the matter. It is the law of heredity at work. Someone had to move us out of Adam (the First Man) and into Christ (the Second Man). Adam could offer his descendants nothing but death, but Christ could offer His descendants life. If humanity could be disconnected from Adam and connected to Christ, then life would be the inheritance instead of death that came from Adam. And this is precisely what God has done. He decided and placed humanity (each of us) into Christ. "But it is [from] Him that *you are in Christ Jesus*" (1 Corinthians 1:30) and "Now He who *establishes us with you in Christ* and anointed us is God" (2 Corinthians 1:21). And based upon the principle of heredity, that which Christ did, was attributed to those who are in Christ's heredity. And now for another shocker: When did God place you in Christ? God elected and decided to place you in Christ before the foundation of the world. "Just as *He chose us in Him* before the foundation of the world, that we would be holy and blameless before Him" (2 Corinthians 1:21).

Stated differently, Adam was the first man, and Jesus was the Second Man as well as the last Adam. With regard to spiritual heredity, there are only two options—being in Adam or being in Christ. Being in Adam resulted in death, while being in Christ results in life. Because God is Love and Love desires abundant life for us, He chose to move us from being in Adam and to place us in Christ so that we could have and receive abundant life. Adam had nothing to offer humanity; Jesus had everything to offer humanity. Accordingly, God, in His Love and mercy, decided to place all of humanity in Christ.

I trust that I have shown convincingly and conclusively that God placed you in Christ. God sovereignly decided to place you *in*

*Christ*. Your behavior and your actions did not place you in Christ, and your behavior and your actions will not keep you from being and remaining *in Christ*. Now let's address the very specific benefits that come from being in Christ. As a result of being in Christ, at least four very distinct things occurred: you were crucified with Christ, you were buried with Christ, you were raised or resurrected with Christ, and you were seated with Christ. Each of these actions is in the past tense. Religious traditions have often explained these consequences of being in Christ by looking for each of them to be fulfilled or completed in the future, but the verb tense makes it clear that in each instance the action has been completed. In addition, God's works—including placing us in Christ and the results mentioned above—were finished from the foundations of the world (Hebrews 4:3). As a result, God has never been anxious with regard to His plans, and He is not anxious with regard to His plan for you.

## GOD CAUSED US TO BE CRUCIFIED WITH CHRIST AND BURIED WITH CHRIST

Because you were in Christ from the foundations of the world, based upon the law of heredity explained above, you were in Christ when He was crucified, which means that you (or more specifically your old Adamic man) were crucified with Christ when He was crucified. This statement is absolutely and clearly declared in Scripture. Revelation 13:8 tells us that "Christ was the lamb who was slain from the creation of the world." Galatians 2:20 says it this way, "I have been crucified with Christ; and it is no longer I who live, but Christ lives in me; and the life which I now live in the flesh I live by faith in the Son of God, who loved me and gave Himself up for me." While Jesus's death is often stated to be substitutionary, it is really more than substitutionary, because the "death of your old man" was accomplished in you and for you because you were present at the crucifixion by being in Christ.

These words "being crucified with" are only recorded five times in the New Testament. Three of these instances are in

Matthew 27:44, Mark 15:32, and John 19:32 and refer to the two thieves who were crucified with Christ. We know that the thieves on either side of the cross were crucified in proximity of time and in proximity of space or location. And the same Greek word is used to describe our crucifixion with Christ, but with even stronger language. In Galatians 2:20, "being crucified with" is all one Greek word for Paul, similar in English to "being co-crucified." This again confirms the greater spiritual reality of this co-crucifixion with Christ. Every bit as much as the thieves were present physically in time and location when Christ was crucified, we were present spiritually in time and location when Christ was crucified. And since the Spiritual is eternal and the most real part of our being, being crucified together spiritually with Christ when he was crucified is of greater reality than the physical reality of the thieves who were crucified together with Christ in time and location. (2 Corinthians 4:18: "[W]hile we look not at the things which are seen, but at the things which are not seen; for the things which are seen are temporal, but the things which are not seen are eternal.")

Paul further describes it in Romans 6:6: "knowing this, that our old [man] was crucified with Him, in order that *our body of sin might be done away with, so that we would no longer be slaves to sin*." Notice that our crucifixion with Christ is not for the purpose of forgiving our sins, but in order that we will become free from and no longer be slaves to the power of sin. Our crucifixion in Christ also freed us from the power of sin and death. As announced in Hebrews 2:14, we further see that Christ's crucifixion and resurrection destroyed "the *one who has the power of death, that is, the devil.*" By destroying the one who had the power of death—the devil—Jesus also totally and completed destroyed the power of death. This is beginning to sound like a total and complete deliverance over sin and death, which is Good News. Andrew Rillera describes it as follows: "The cross is not the precondition for God's forgiveness. Rather, it is what proves how unrelenting God's Love is, even for God's enemies. And humanity is being saved, not from God, but from Sin and Death."[1] Romans 6 is the

---

1. Rillera, 268—269.

consummate passage that fully sets forth the amazing concepts of being in Christ in His death, burial, and resurrection.

> Or do you not know that all of us who have been baptized into Christ Jesus have been baptized into His death? ⁴Therefore we have been buried with Him through baptism into death, so that, just as Christ was raised from the dead through the glory of the Father, so we too may walk in newness of life. ⁵For if we have become united with Him in the likeness of His death, certainly we shall also be His resurrection, ⁶knowing this, that our old [man] was crucified with Him, in order that our body of sin might be done away with, so that we would no longer be slaves to sin; ⁷for the one who has died is freed from sin. ⁸Now if we have died with Christ, we believe that we shall also live with Him (Romans 6:3–8).

Verse 3 states that we have been baptized into His death. To help us understand this concept, consider that water baptism is simply an outward recognition that we were baptized into His death by being crucified with Him. Water baptism does not place us in Christ. By baptism, we express faith that God has already placed us in Christ—including in His crucifixion—and we therefore express that faith outwardly through water baptism. I see a common component to baptism and circumcision: just as circumcision did not do a substantive work, but rather was a sign, water baptism also does not do a substantive work, but is simply a sign of belief and trust in the decision and work that God graciously completed. Romans 4:11: "And he received the sign of circumcision, a seal of the righteousness that he had by faith while he was still uncircumcised." We see that circumcision was not creative, but was a sign of what had already occurred, and the same is true for baptism. For some of you, that just could be the straw that breaks the camel's back, but I hope you will hang in here with me. Water baptism cannot accomplish what has already been accomplished and what has been true since the foundations of the world. But water baptism is a beautiful allegory of the fact that you were crucified, buried, and resurrected with Christ. It is so beautiful that I decided I wanted to be baptized again in 2012 after coming to the revelation that I had been crucified with Christ from the beginning of creation. My first baptism was obligatory; my second baptism was revelatory.

## GOD RAISED US WITH CHRIST

According to Romans 6:5, we "shall also be His resurrection." This is the victory of being in Christ; we suffered crucifixion, death, and burial so that we could be raised again for a new life; a life that is no longer a slave to the power of sin. Colossians 3:1 "Therefore, if you have been raised with Christ, keep seeking the things that are above, where Christ is, seated at the right hand of God." And the pinnacle of this plan is that the old Adamic man has died, and we are resurrected a new man who is in Christ and seated with Christ. 2 Corinthians 5:17 "Therefore, if anyone is in Christ, he is a new creation; the old has gone, the new has come!" This promise of being a new creation is not something yet to be fulfilled; this promise of being a new creation is something to be believed and received, even when it looks unbelievable. Why believe the unbelievable? Because God's words are not limited by logic, circumstances, or even seemingly impossibility. For greater understanding, let's look at the angel's words to Mary and her response.

> And the angel said to her, "Do not be afraid, Mary, for you have found favor with God. [32]And behold, you will conceive in your womb and give birth to a son, and you shall name Him Jesus." [34]But Mary said to the angel, "How will this be, since I am a virgin?" [38]And Mary said, "Behold, the Lord's bond-servant; may it be done to me according to your word." And the angel departed from her (Luke 1:31-32, 34, and 38).

Mary believed in spite of the fact it seemed impossible. There is an internal conflict in most Christians. It is a conflict of understanding versus trusting. The things of the Spirit (the power of the Kingdom) do not manifest by understanding but by believing and trusting. Therefore, if we substitute understanding for trusting, we will not receive. Understanding is not bad in any regard. However, if we substitute understanding for trusting, or if we insist on understanding before we trust, then it is like trying to run a car on water—there is no power in it. Understanding and trusting are a great combination. But understanding should never be a prerequisite for trusting and believing. Mary said, "How can this be?" but then she also said, "Be it unto me according to your word." Just as you were crucified with Christ, you also are His resurrection. It is not necessary to understand how you become His resurrection in order for it to be true.

Mary's response to the angel has often played through my mind and had a profound effect upon my heart for the last few years. In hindsight, it was God preparing me to receive His word to me even when it seemed impossible. Let me give you a personal example of believing God's promise even when it seemed unbelievable, that I experienced while in Uganda with a team from Christ Fellowship in December 2022. In response to a group listening prayer exercise, which was basically for the benefit of the missionaries with whom we were working, I asked the Lord to reveal a lie that I believed about myself or God. Immediately, I heard and confessed what God brought to my heart—that I felt like I was a disappointment to God; specifically, that "God was disappointed with me." Recognizing that God had graciously identified the lie, I released it to Jesus, and I visualized a dove on Jesus's shoulder carrying the lie away. That thought (which was a lie) was like a bubble that burst and disappeared, just like water evaporates on a hot day.

I asked Jesus what truth He wanted me to know to replace the lie. God responded, "You could NEVER be a disappointment to me." I saw the words appear before me, and I saw NEVER in all caps. I started to debate with God, because from my understanding of my past and even my present, I did not understand how it could be true that I could NEVER be a disappointment to God. I said, "How can it be" (just like Mary did), but remembered that Mary also said, "Nevertheless be it to me according to what God has said." Then I felt God encourage me to receive his word to me by faith or trust, just like Mary had done, even though it seemed to me that it could not be true. That was the challenge I felt in order to receive. And by His grace, I was empowered to believe what seemed unbelievable. Ultimately, God's words to me are more true than my feelings, and they often transcend rational understanding. I do not understand it, but I receive it. This is how I encourage you to receive the truth that you have been resurrected with Christ, or as Paul says in Romans 6, "you have become his resurrection." I love the way that Andrew Rillera summarizes this incredible spiritual work. "What we have in Hebrews, then, is the notion of double participation. First, the Son of God participates in the full experience of humanity by even tasting death so that, second, humanity is enabled to participate in his death and resurrection to indestructible."[2]

## GOD SEATED US IN HEAVENLY PLACES WITH CHRIST

Just as icing on the cake of this Good News, I want to point out that we are also seated in heavenly places with Christ right now. Ephesians 2:5–6: [God who is rich in mercy], "made us alive with Christ even when we were dead in transgressions—it is by grace you have been saved. And God raised us up with Christ and seated us with him in the heavenly realms in Christ Jesus." Again, I want to point out the past tense of the verb. Perhaps I will understand the implications of currently being seated with Christ later in my life, but I do know that it is a spiritual reality, notwithstanding how unbelievable it may seem and notwithstanding my further lack of understanding.

To summarize, it is God who placed us in Christ before the foundation of the world so that the old man would be crucified and so that we would be raised a new man that was part of a new lineage; that we would be in Christ rather than in Adam. Romans 7 is a more thorough explanation of how death, which occurred when we were crucified with Christ, sets us free from the law, and Paul uses the law regarding marriage as an example of how death frees us from the law. Being crucified in Christ set us free from Adam's lineage, and being resurrected with Christ placed us in Jesus's lineage as a new creation.

2. Rillera, 240.

# Chapter 9

## Who Was Included in Christ?
*Does All Mean All?*

SCRIPTURE CONFIRMS THAT CHRIST chose us to be in Him before the foundation of the world. But this leads to another question: "Who was included in Christ?" Who does "us" include? Was it everyone?

Let me begin by asking you a question. Who is more powerful, Adam or Jesus? Did Jesus overcome all the power and effects of sin, or is there an aspect of Adam's sin that Jesus could not defeat? Are there men or women who inherited death through Adam that Jesus will not rescue? Are there men or women who inherited death through Adam that Jesus cannot rescue? Our theological answer would, of course, be that Jesus is greater, but the answers to the above questions may actually indicate that we believe Adam's sin was more powerful than Christ's redemption. To answer these questions, let's begin with Romans 5:12, 17–19:

> Therefore, just as through one man sin entered into the world, and death through sin, and so death spread to all mankind, because all sinned. . . . $^{17}$For if by the offense of the one, death reigned through the one, much more will those who receive the abundance of grace and of the

gift of righteousness reign in life through the One, Jesus Christ. ¹⁸So then, as through one offense [to] condemnation to all mankind, so also through one act of righteousness [to] justification of life to all mankind. ¹⁹For as through the one man's disobedience the many were made sinners, so also through the obedience of the One the many will be made righteous.

And we must also consider 1 Corinthians 15:21–22: "For since by a man death came, by a Man also came the resurrection of the dead. For as in Adam all die, so also in [Messiah] all will be made alive."

These verses state that because Adam, the First Man, sinned, death reigned in the lives of all his descendants, which is all of mankind. As confusing as it may be to understand and as unfair as it may seem, we all readily accept this spiritual truth. But the point of the verse is not to bemoan the detrimental effects of Adam's sin, of which we are very well aware, but to proclaim the comparative, and yet fully redemptive, overcoming work of Christ. These passages compare the consequences of one act of sin to the consequences of one act of obedience by Christ, which brought justification or righteousness to all mankind.

When someone preaches that we were all in Adam and all sinned, there is complete agreement. I can hear the "*amens*." No one objects to the bad news. However, we often do not accept the good news that just as we were all in Adam, we were also all in Christ. In fact, I have heard sincere believers state unequivocally that "all" means everyone (all of humanity) in Romans 5:12, but that in Romans 5:18, "all" means the elect. Obviously, this includes a component of predestination, but it seems particularly illogical that the same Greek word used in Romans 5:12, means something different when used in Romans 5:18. This disagreement about "all" in Romans 5:18 focused me on a couple of tasks, which paid amazing dividends for my insight and understanding.

First, I re-read all of the New Testament looking for passages that indicate that Jesus redeemed all men and passages that indicate limited atonement or predestination. Generally, I found no verses that indicated limited atonement, but there were several verses concerning or suggesting predestination. Predestination has been accepted or rejected on extremes rather than recognizing that both predestination and free will can exist in harmony. For those who have embraced the concept of predestination, it often results in a rationale that there must be limited atonement; otherwise, all would be justified, an unacceptable conclusion and application because it is too good to be true, and it sounds too much like universalism. The thinking is that if justification is by grace and grace alone, then grace must be limited; otherwise, everyone will be a recipient. However, you will not find any verses specifically stating that atonement includes less than the whole world. It is simply necessary to infer limited atonement based upon the assumption that God would choose fewer than everyone to be His children.

In the first instance, this violates the foundational truths that God is kind, good, and loving. In fact, it describes a deity that is unsafe and unpredictable, that prefers power and control over Love. While we cannot deny that Scripture includes concepts of predestination, my understanding is that predestination can exist with universal atonement without the necessity of making atonement less than full and complete. I believe they co-exist by stating that our choices are not predetermined or predestined (and therefore the consequences of our choices are not predetermined or predestined), meaning that we retain a measure of free will and decision making, but our status as forgiven, righteous, accepted, loved, and beloved children of God is predetermined and nothing can change that.

Paul's message to the Thessalonians was similar: "For God has not destined us for wrath, but for obtaining salvation through our Lord Jesus Christ" (1 Thessalonians 5:9). Just as Jesus was predetermined to be nailed to the cross for our complete freedom,[1] we were also predestined to salvation, meaning "deliverance, preservation, and salvation." Also, God has predetermined and predestined

---

1. Acts 2:23 "this Man, delivered over by the *predetermined* plan and foreknowledge of God, you nailed to a cross by the hands of godless men and put Him to death."

that He will never leave us or forsake us. We are predestined to never be separated from Him, even though subjectively we too often wrongly conclude that we are separated.

Salvation or sanctification is simply the process of aligning our beliefs and our actions with our predestined status as forgiven, righteous, accepted, loved, and beloved children of God. And here is the most amazing of all facts: no matter what bad decisions we make, no matter how many wrong paths we go down, no matter how often we choose independence from God over dependence upon God, no matter how many times we deny Him, no matter how many times we wander away like a stray sheep, no matter how often we end up in the pigpen, He works in each and every one of these decisions to bring about His will, which is our salvation. We never make a decision so bad or so big that it impacts, changes, or hinders our predetermined status as forgiven, righteous, accepted, loved, and beloved children of God. I hope you are beginning to see this as Good News for everyone. It isn't Good News for a certain group, but not Good News for a different group. It is Good News for all.

The verses that point to the fact that God redeemed all mankind are numerous. In isolation, none of the verses should be ignored, but when considered in totality, the verses paint a different picture than what modern evangelicalism has described about the Good News. The following are several of the verses I consider most astounding and significant for this topic.

- John 1:7, 9 He came as a witness that he might bear witness of the light, *that all might believe through him.* ⁹There was the true light, which, coming into the world, *enlightens every man.*

- Acts 3:26 "God raised up His Servant for you first, and sent Him to bless you by turning *every one of you* from your wicked ways."

- Romans 5:18 consequently, just as one trespass resulted in condemnation for all people, so also one righteous act resulted *in justification and life for all people.*

- Romans 6:10 For the death that He died, He died to sin, *once for all;* but the life that He lives, He lives to God.

- Romans 8:29-30 *For those God foreknew* (meaning "to know beforehand," which is everyone) he also predestined to be conformed to the image of his Son, that he might be the firstborn among many brothers and sisters. And those he predestined, he also called; those he called, he also justified; those he justified, he also glorified.

- Romans 11:32 For God has bound everyone over to disobedience so that he may have mercy on them all.

- 2 Corinthians 5:14-15 For Christ's love compels us, because we are convinced that one died for all, and therefore all died [in Christ]. And he died for all, that those who live should no longer live for themselves but for him who died for them and was raised again.

- Colossians 1:28 We proclaim Him, admonishing every person [3956] and teaching every [3956] person with all [3956] wisdom, so that we may present every person [3956] complete [perfect] in Christ.

- 1 Timothy 2:5-6 For there is one God and one mediator between God and mankind, the man Christ Jesus, who gave himself as a ransom for all people.

- Timothy 4:10 That is why we labor and strive, because we have put our hope in the living God, who is the Savior of all people, and especially of those who believe.

- 1 John 2:2 and He Himself is the propitiation for our sins; and not for ours only, but also for the sins of the whole world.

Would you read the above verses again? Will you read them slowly and meditate on what each verse is communicating? You just cannot explain away the concepts of "all" and "every person," which are the same Greek word. There are no concepts in these verses (or any other verses) that God atones for the sins of a portion of the world. Given our current evangelical thinking, that men and women must believe and comply with the proper process in order to be justified, I find that 1 Timothy 4:10 completely dismantles that thought process. "That is why we labor and strive, because we have put our hope in the living God, who *is the Savior of all people, and especially of those who believe.*"

I actually do not know that I can offer anything additional with regard to the conversation that God has redeemed everyone. The Scripture speaks clearly, loudly, and convincingly! If you still doubt, I would challenge you to search the Bible to find a passage that says Christ redeemed less than the whole of humanity. I may be wrong in my conclusions, but once I started this process, as best as I knew how to do so, I put away my conclusions of what I wanted Scripture to say and asked the Living Word to reveal the fullness of the Gospel to me. And so many of my perceived notions and traditions started to fall away. In fairness to the current reader, if someone handed me this manuscript 20 years ago, I would have quickly labeled the conclusions as heretical, just proving the gentleness, faithfulness, and patience of God in revealing His heart and the Good News to me.

In support of the argument of limited atonement, I have heard it explained that not all of humanity is God's children, only those who were created for redemption and justification—or, in some theological approaches, only those who were predestined are God's children. In May 2024, Diane and I visited Greece on a Footsteps of Paul tour. We stood at the Areopagus near the Parthenon where Paul preached the sermon at Mars Hill. The Areopagus was the location where Athenians and visitors would spend their time talking about new ideas. You might call them a think tank or a bunch of philosophers. Apparently, they did not have jobs to attend, and before social media, they entertained themselves with debate and discussion. In the same location where Paul spoke to the men of Athens, our tour guide read Acts 17:22–34, and I heard something that I had never heard before. But first, how successful was Paul at converting the Athenians? Verse 34 tells us that some men and a woman believed the message, but the others did not believe. Although Paul had great debate skills, he was unable to persuade most of them to believe, because debate is not the pathway to believing; revelation, which leads to faith, is the pathway to believing. But now to the main point. In addressing the whole crowd, including a majority who would not believe, Paul identifies all of them as "children of God." "Being then *the children of God*, we ought not to think that the Divine Nature is like gold or silver or stone, an image formed by the art and thought of man" (Acts 17:29 NASB95). Paul refers to those who will reject the Gospel as "children of God." The believers are the children of God, and the unbelievers are the children of God. Now that is Good News worth sharing with the unbeliever and the not-yet-believer. Rather than trying to convert someone to our theology by telling them that if they do not become God's children that God will separate from them, try telling them they are already God's beloved child and God desires for them to start living according to who they are.

You may be asking if I am suggesting that all roads lead to God or that every road leads to heaven? I absolutely do not believe that any of our roads lead to God or to heaven. I firmly believe Jesus's response to Thomas in John 14:6, "I am the way, and the truth, and the life; no one comes to the Father except through Me." To me, that means that none of our "ways"—our rituals, processes, methods, and efforts—bring us to God, but I do believe that God did everything for everyone so that every person may receive abundant life. When I hear the question *"Are you saying that all roads lead to God,"* it often actually indicates an underlying belief that your road is the right road and all the other roads are wrong. If your road is right, then there's a better chance that my road is not the right way. The question or dilemma itself is often elicited from fear that if I do not practice the right process, then I could spend eternity in hell. We often have a vested interest in other people's roads being wrong so that there is a greater chance that our road is the only correct way.

But Jesus is the way; Jesus is the only road. Are you ok with the fact that God rescues people who do not follow your process? Does it offend you if God rescues people who do not follow your way, your process, or your ritual? If you are offended, you are not alone. Our tendency is to be offended when others receive what we thought we worked hard to obtain. Isn't that the message of the parable of the workers in the vineyard in Matthew 20? Look at the workers' response in verses 11 and 12: "When they received it, they grumbled at the landowner, [12]saying, 'These who were hired last worked only one hour, and you have made them equal to us who have borne the burden of the day's work and the scorching heat.'" This parable highlights God's grace and generosity. As you might imagine based upon a description of previously living from an earning approach, I found this parable quite offensive until one day the Lord spoke to my heart and said, "If you are offended by this parable, it is an indication that grace also offends you."

The fact that God has done everything is actually more fully aligned with "*no one comes to the father except through Jesus*" than most of our evangelical theories, which proscribe a particular process or a specific ritual or a certain kind of prayer, or a certain method of baptism, or a certain process for communion. Do you realize that people do not have to be aware that they are coming to God through Jesus in order to be found by God and to come to God in the way that Jesus made? They do not have to be praying to Jesus in order for Jesus to find them. They do not have to realize that Jesus made the way in order to receive the wholeness and life that Jesus provided. That is another aspect of the Good News.

God finds us even when we are on our own path, and isn't that glorious because *none of our own paths lead to God*. Paul is certainly an example of God finding him when he was on his own path. Paul's conversion expresses this principle, and he confirmed the concept when he quoted Isaiah in Romans 10:20, "'And Isaiah is very bold and says, "I WAS FOUND BY THOSE WHO DID NOT SEEK ME, I REVEALED MYSELF TO THOSE WHO DID NOT ASK FOR ME."'"

Of course, your next question is, "Are you saying that all humans go to heaven?" At this point, you may contemplate that I don't generally divide humans into a linear line of those going to heaven and those going to hell. I would divide humans into those who are living in the truth that they are God's beloved children and those who are living under a lie that they are not loved or living under a lie that they have been forsaken. The preceding discussion has been a conversation on justification (i.e. righteousness), not the afterlife. Honestly, I do not know how the above interrelates to the afterlife. The afterlife includes pieces of the entire puzzle that I do not endeavor to address here because I have very limited insight. Hell and fire are outside the purpose of this writing, but there are other scholarly resources on the topic of hell that I found helpful. I will remind you, however, that in the NASB20, *hell* is not mentioned once in Acts or any of Paul's writings.

I do know that there is a hell. I do know that many people are currently living a life of hell because they do not trust the One who loves them the most. If you find yourself in a living hell, you can know for certain that God has not abandoned you and will not abandon you. "For you will not abandon my soul to hades, nor will you allow your Holy One to undergo decay" (Acts 2:27). But I also know that God never ceases to be Love or to act lovingly. I do know that with God, everything is redemptive, even an experience in hell. I do know that there is almost nothing in Scripture that tells us that natural death cuts off the opportunity to receive and trust God. I do know that God is not limited by time. I do know that God has all the time He needs.

In God's economy, there is enough time. As mentioned above, I know some of you will feel the necessity of having an answer to the question *"what happens if you die without accepting or receiving God's forgiveness?"* But perhaps we should trust what Scripture clearly reveals regarding justification and forgiveness while embracing the mystery of what has not been revealed regarding the afterlife. As Christians, we have made too many assumptions about the afterlife and discounted God's Love and patience. More importantly, I do know that atonement was and is universal; that God has forgiven all the sins of humanity from Adam until the end of time, which launches us into the next focus of this chapter.

As stated earlier, we often believe more in the power of Adam to bring death than we believe in the power of Jesus to bring new life. We have more confidence in the power of death than in the power of life. But Jesus is the last Adam and the second man. Jesus is mankind's chance to change heredity; to get into Christ and out of Adam. Jesus is mankind's opportunity and way to move from an inheritance of death to an inheritance of life.

It is worth repeating the question, "Who is more powerful, Adam or Jesus?" And it is worth repeating what we really believe, notwithstanding our professed creeds. We believe more in the power of being in Adam than we believe in the power of being in Christ. We have forgotten about and overlooked Romans 3:24. The evangelical church has built its message around Romans 3:23, but neglected Romans 3:24, which is equally applicable and directed to the same "all" of humanity referenced in verse 23. "For *all* have sinned and fall short of the glory of God, [24]*being justified* as a gift by His grace through the redemption which is in Christ Jesus." "All" is an amazing and inclusive concept.

Did Jesus's crucifixion, death, and resurrection pay for the sins of all mankind? If not, then He did not fully overcome the works of the enemy, and He did not completely overcome the effects of sin. That would make Him an incomplete Savior. 1 John 2:2 "and He Himself is the propitiation for our sins; and not for ours only, but also for those of the whole world." (See also Romans 5:18.) If Jesus paid for the sins of all humanity, is all of humanity forgiven without any effort or action on the individual's part? Suppose I go to the bank and pay off your mortgage. In that case, you are debt-free even if you don't know it (lack of knowledge) or even if you don't accept it (rebellion or independence) because the debt is objectively determined by the bank, not determined by the debtor.

Try going to the bank and endeavoring to convince the bank that your debt is paid off because you feel it is true. Your feelings will not persuade the bank; the bank will look to objective evidence. That is also true if I pay off your debt, but you go to the bank and try to make a payment on your debt because you feel the debt is due. The bank will not be persuaded by your feelings in that instance either; the bank will once again look to objective evidence. Whether our sins are forgiven is a decision of the forgiver (God), not us. If the debt has been paid, there is no longer any penalty that can be imposed for non-payment of the debt. But you, as the debtor, can make a subjective decision about the debt and live subjectively as if you are a debtor while objectively you are not. In other words, the bank will not and legally cannot foreclose on your debt (because it does not exist), but you can live in fear of foreclosure.

For me, the real personal question for each of us is not whether we are forgiven and justified, it is whether we are living in the truth that we are forgiven or not living in the truth that we are forgiven. Does our subjective truth affect who God says we are, or just our perception of who we think we are? Does our subjective truth affect our status before God? Can we be forgiven and not believe or receive it? Absolutely!

Does not believing change the reality of what God has done? Absolutely not! We are forgiven, but because of our failure to believe the truth, we live as if we are unforgiven. This does not break into an easy distinction between "Christian" and "non-Christian." In fact, most of my Christian life, I lived as if I were not fully or completely forgiven. I know many sincere Christians who live from a place of being uncertain about their relationship with God and unsure that all their sins (or their next sins) are or will be forgiven. Are the Christians who have said the right prayer fully forgiven, even though they do not believe that they are and even though they lack security in their righteousness? There are plenty of questions above that you can ask God about. He is not afraid of or intimidated by your questions. He will be kind and patient with you! He has been kind and patient with me!

Stated another way: Does free will affect who you are or only how you live? To respond to the question further, let's consider that Jesus was crucified with two thieves on either side of the cross. To one, Jesus said, "Today you will be with me in paradise." We assume Jesus meant and intended that the other thief would not be with Him. Let me repeat, we assume Jesus meant and intended that the other thief would not be with Him. But let's not assume; let's search and explore. Based upon our doctrines, we imply that the other thief will not be in paradise. But Jesus did not tell the second thief that; we have read that into the conversation because it fit the story as it was told to us. One thief, who received the words that Jesus spoke, lived his final hours in peace and security, because in believing Jesus's words, he received what God had always planned for him, and it gave him security to face death. The other thief lived his final hours without peace and security because he did not believe Jesus's words. Therefore, failing to believe certainly affected how they lived. And it affected how they faced death, as well as how they entered death. And honestly, we have almost no indication of what occurred after their deaths.

Let's spend some more time talking about the concept of "all." Does "all" actually mean "all"? If you are convinced that "all" means "all," then you may want to skip ahead. If you are not convinced, the following will be technical but instructive. The Greek word for all (G3956 "pas") means "each, every, any, all, the whole, everyone, all things, everything." This is a very inclusive and clear definition. However, there is a second Greek word translated as all (G3745 "hosos") which means "as great as, as far as, how much, how many, whoever." By definition, the latter Greek word does not include everyone or all, but by definition, the former (G3956 "pas") does include all. The first step is to determine which Greek word is in the original. "Hosos" occurs 115 times in the New Testament, while "pas" occurs 1,243 times in the New Testament. The NASB20 translates the Hebrew words and the Greek words as "all" 5,215 times in 4,376 verses.

With regard to the 1,243 occurrences of "pas" in the New Testament, to determine if the word is used consistently with the general definition, you must examine the context. The context will generally clarify whether "all" means "everyone" or whether "all" means a portion of the whole. In some instances, "all" refers to a group, like "all of the chief priests and the elders." In those instances, it is clear that "all" does not refer to all of the Israelites and especially not all of humanity. This is usually clear from the context. Therefore, it was necessary to read through every one (all) of the 4,376 verses for clarity. I never found any instance where "all" should be construed to be less than everyone, except for those instances where the context clearly limited the application, like "all of the chief priests and elders." I know this sounds tedious and technical, but it is in response to a doctrinal position that "all" means "all" in Romans 5:12, but that it does not mean "all" in Romans 5:18 and 1 Corinthians 15:22. If "all" does not mean "all" in Romans 5:18 and 1 Corinthians 15:22, then does it actually mean "all" in any of the passages? Below are a few verses that I found most instructive.[2]

- Luke 20:38 "Now He is not the God of the dead, but of the living; for all [3956] live to Him."
- John 1:7 He came as a witness, to testify about the Light, so that all [3956] might believe through him.
- John 1:9 This was the true Light that, coming into the world, enlightens every [3956] person.
- John 1:16 For of His fullness we have all [3956] received, and grace upon grace.
- Romans 4:16 For this reason it is by faith, in order that it may be in accordance with grace, so that the promise will be guaranteed to all [3956] the descendants, not only to those who are of the Law, but also to those who are of the faith of Abraham, who is the father of us all [3956],
- Romans 8:32 He who did not spare His own Son, but delivered Him over for us all [3956], how will He not also with Him freely give us all [3956] things.
- Romans 11:32 For God has shut up all [3956] in disobedience, so that He may show mercy to all [3956].
- 1 Corinthians 12:13 For by one Spirit we were all [3956] baptized into one body, whether Jews or Greeks, whether slaves or free, and we were all [3956] made to drink of one Spirit.
- Ephesians 4:6 one God and Father of all [3956] who is over all [3956] and through all [3956] and in all [3956].

2. Attached is an Appendix B with each and every one (all) of the verses that I found relevant.

- 1 Timothy 2:6 who gave Himself as a ransom for all [3956], the testimony given at the proper time.

- Titus 2:11 For the grace of God has appeared, bringing salvation to all [3956] people,

- Hebrews 2:9 But we do see Him who was made for a little while lower than the angels, namely, Jesus, because of His suffering death crowned with glory and honor, so that by the grace of God He might taste death [experience] for everyone [3956].

- 1 John 2:2 and He Himself is the propitiation for our sins; and not for ours only, but also for the sins of the whole [3956] world.

Once again, I ask you to reread the above verses, or better yet, each of the verses in Appendix B. The verses above do not include the verses that I have already referenced, which are even more direct and profound. My logical mind and my understanding of God's heart cannot fathom any other conclusion than "all" really does mean "all" in Romans 5:12, but also in Romans 5:18 and 1 Corinthians 15:22. That conclusion is supported by the text itself, but also by the entirety of Scripture.

I graduated from the Marshall-Wythe School of Law at the College of William and Mary in 1986. By the way, law school was a profoundly spiritual time when I responded to God's invitation to seek Him. Law school is a different style of learning in which you use case books rather than textbooks. The case books in law school are not in outline form. A case book does not lay out the law in an area in a systematic or sequential approach. You read one case and then another case and then another case, and you formulate what the law is by putting all the cases together.

Years ago, I realized that the Bible is more like a case book than a textbook. There is story after story, and we ask the Holy Spirit to put them together. If we take them in isolation (like the Pharisees did), we can form a theological position that is inconsistent with the whole. We end up developing rules and regulations that destroy people rather than give life. A great example of this is taking the story of the rich young ruler in isolation and interpreting it to mean that each of us has to sell everything we have and own to follow Christ, but the entirety of Scripture tells a different story. Therefore, while I am encouraging a reasonable interpretation of Romans 5:18 and 1 Corinthians 15:22, I am also encouraging that we look at the whole of Scripture comprehensively. That is why I have quoted so many Bible verses. The evidence is overwhelming. However, men and women are not persuaded by evidence, but by the Spirit of Truth. By now, I trust that I have at least generated a question in your heart, and all I can do is ask that you talk to God about your questions, your concerns, and even your frustrations. And I would encourage that you hold to the unshakeable, absolute truths that God is Love, God is kind, God is good, and that God will never ever leave us or separate from us.

But we are not quite finished. There is still more that God has done for us!

# Chapter 10

# God Broke the Power of Sin and Death

As described earlier, there is a difference between sins and the power of sin. Even though our sins are forgiven, unless the power or force of sin is dealt with, we simply keep repeating our failures, and this is not the highest form of life. This was an expectation in the Levitical law, as there were regularly scheduled times of offering sacrifices for sins, because there was the expectation that sins would continue. Our deep-rooted tracks of beliefs and choices exert a power over us until we realize that not only are our sins forgiven, but that through Christ, the power of sin, the irresistible draw of sin, was also broken. As we see this additional aspect of Christ's work, the Gospel expands in provision and effect. In addition, as referenced earlier, Romans 6:23 confirms that the most severe consequence of sin is death: "For the wages of sin is death, but the gracious gift of God is eternal life in Christ Jesus our Lord." Therefore, although our sins have been forgiven, if the power of death is not broken, our sins, although forgiven, give death the power to rule over us. Something or someone had to break the power of sin and the power of death. Jesus's crucifixion and resurrection were actually the provision that broke the power of sin and death. Jesus was fully aware of what He was accomplishing, which is why He declared with His last breath, "It is finished!"[1]

Revisiting Romans 6:6, we see that Christ was crucified and that we were crucified with Him "in order that our body of sin might be done away with, so that we would no longer be slaves to sin." *Notice that our crucifixion with Christ is not for the purpose of forgiving our sins*, but in order that we will become free from and no longer be slaves to the power of sin. Our crucifixion in Christ is to free us from the power of sin and death, which freedom is accomplished when we are resurrected in Christ and moved out from being in Adam. The amazing truth of this work is that it was accomplished in God's heart before the creation of the world and completed in time on the cross. In Adam, the power of sin controls you. In Christ, you are no longer a slave of sin. A slave must submit to his/her master, but when you are in Christ, you have a new master, Christ, and you are no longer a slave to sin. Sin can no longer command you, but it can still convince you or deceive you. Lies and deception are the only means left to prevent you from accepting and believing who you really are. When you are in Adam (death), sin reigns, and when you are in Christ (righteousness), grace reigns (see Romans 5:21). God's and Christ's obedience and submission move you from being in Adam to being in Christ, which breaks the power of sin and death so that sin can no longer control and dictate to you as a master can control and dictate to his slave.

You may be questioning why Jesus died a brutal death of crucifixion if our sins were already forgiven. Jesus was not crucified to appease the Father's wrath so that He could forgive us. Jesus was not the penal substitution so that God could forgive us. God did not need the cross or Jesus's crucifixion in order to forgive us. Love would never require a payment or sacrifice in order to forgive. Biblically, we are instructed to forgive others. Still, we never require the person whom we need to forgive to offer some form of

---

1. "Therefore when Jesus had received the sour wine, He said, 'It is finished!' And He bowed His head and gave up His spirit" (John 19:30).

sacrifice or appeasement in order to permit or empower our forgiveness of them. We freely give forgiveness without any payment or any condition. In every instance in Scripture and every instance of counseling with someone, forgiveness is always presented as a unilateral transaction, never a bilateral transaction. How could God (who is the most kind, compassionate, loving person ever) require a sacrifice or payment in order to forgive when his sons and daughters are instructed to forgive without requiring a sacrifice or anything in return?

Jesus was therefore crucified so that we would experience death and resurrection with Him, so that we would be born again, free from the power of sin and the power of death. Peter describes it as follows: "and He Himself brought our sins in His body up on the cross, *so that we might die to sin* and live for righteousness." Peter is not referring to the forgiveness of our sins, but to the truth that we were freed from the power of sin.

About the same time that God ruined my legalistic prayer life, I began to get a very faint understanding of this concept, but I was not ready to concede that God did not require Jesus's death to forgive our sins. Penal substitution had been ingrained in me too much, and it was not even a consideration at that time. Even contemplating it was heretical. At this point, it may even seem heretical for you to read such words. Nevertheless, the concept was a tiny little seed that has continued to grow and mature. For many years at Easter, our family hosted an Easter celebration at our home. We would invite 20 or more families and have up to 100 children and parents. Everyone brought snacks and Easter candy. After a short devotion with the whole group, our family did a little skit with the kids while parents were hiding eggs, prizes, and candy. It was a blessed time of fun and fellowship, and an annual way to maintain connection with friends.

One Easter, my short devotions consisted of stating that the traditional explanation of the reason for Easter—that Jesus died to forgive our sins—was incomplete. I explained that such an incomplete description took away from the real significance of the cross. No one threw eggs at me, thankfully. That short devotion was a follow-up to a conversation that Diane and I had with our children. Before that Easter party, we "apologized" to the children that we had explained the sole purpose of Easter was that Jesus died to forgive our sins. We told them it was incomplete. More than 15 years later, I am now seeing that it was incorrect rather than incomplete. The tragedy of being incorrect with regard to penal substitution is that it painted the Father as wrathful, angry, and demanding, totally misrepresenting His heart of Love. As mentioned previously, the entire Christian life is about learning to trust God. But a God that is wrathful, angry, and demanding—a God that demands the death of His Son so that He can forgive humanity's sins—is strikingly opposite of someone that you can trust, thus undermining our invitation to believe and trust God. However, God was so very patient in my process of understanding that penal substitution mistakenly represents His heart and His plan. He will be equally patient in your process.

As you might see, many of my beliefs stand or fall on the truth and proper application of 2 Corinthians 5:19 "namely, that God was in Christ reconciling the world to Himself, not counting their wrongdoings against them," and several similar verses. If it is true and accurate that the Godhead made the decision to forgive all sins of all mankind before the cross or the resurrection, then Jesus was not crucified to appease God's wrath. Jesus was crucified so that all of us, having been placed in Christ by God, would experience death and be resurrected as a new man. It is still absolutely true that Christ was crucified for us, but more true that we were crucified with Christ, and in so doing that we would be buried and resurrected with Him. This is at least part of the meaning and expression of 2 Corinthians 5:17: "Therefore if anyone is in Christ, this person is a new creation; the old things passed away; behold, new things have come." Nice concept, nice verse, but we basically have never really believed this verse is true for ourselves in the present. And we certainly never believed this verse is true for all of humanity. However, God is ready to reveal to you that 2 Corinthians 5:17 is a present reality grounded in God's Love and compassion for you and empowered and given power through you, as well as all humanity, from the fact that you have been crucified with Christ.

If the above is true, then what about I Corinthians 15:3 and 17? What is the proper interpretation and application of 1 Corinthians 15:3: "For I handed down to you as of first importance what I also received, that Christ died for our sins according to the Scriptures," and 1 Corinthians 15:17: "And if Christ has not been raised, your faith is futile; you are still in your sins." I cannot state this for certain, but I do believe "sins" would be better translated as "sin" as in still under the power of sin (Romans 3:9) or as in being the slave of sin (Romans 6:6–7). The Greek word for "sin" and "sins" is the same, as explained earlier, so whether it is translated as "sin" or "sins" is determined by the translator. As I understand it from the discussion above, all of our "sins" were forgiven as a decision of the Godhead, even without the necessity of a blood sacrifice.

But are there Biblical accounts of God forgiving without the necessity of offering a sacrifice? Let's return to Moses's intercession prayer in Numbers 14:19: "Please forgive the guilt of this people in accordance with the greatness of Your mercy, just as You also have forgiven this people, from Egypt even until now." First, Moses realizes and acknowledges that God has faithfully and consistently been forgiving the Israelites since they left Egypt. Moses was well aware of God's willingness and grace to forgive. And just as Moses expected, "So the LORD said, 'I have forgiven them in accordance with your word'" (verse 20). We are visiting this occurrence again because it highlights the fact that forgiveness occurred in the absence of any sacrifice for atonement. Look again at the passage and you will see that Moses offered no sacrifice at all. There is indeed a Biblical example of forgiveness of sins without offering a sacrifice.

Let's also consider David. David lived in the time of the Old Covenant, but appeared to function ahead of his time in the New Covenant under the covenant of grace. According to the Levitical law as set out in Leviticus 24:9, the consecrated showbread was reserved exclusively for the sons of Aaron because it was holy to the Lord. However, when David was running from Saul, he asked Ahimelech the priest for food, but Ahimelech had nothing except the consecrated showbread. Despite the Levitical law, which prohibited David from eating the showbread, he nevertheless ate it and gave it to his men (1 Samuel 21:1-6). David did not offer any sacrifice to atone for his lawlessness, and yet God blessed his efforts. If David sinned (and I do not think that he did), God forgave him. But there was clearly a time when David sinned. In the most well-known but tragic story of David's life, he committed adultery with Bathsheba and ordered the murder of Uriah. Under the law, the only penalty for these sins was death. There were no exceptions and no loopholes to escape the consequences. But look at how the Lord responds to David in 2 Samuel 12:13-14 (NIV): "Then David said to Nathan, 'I have sinned against the Lord.' Nathan replied, 'The Lord has taken away your sin. You are not going to die.'" The Lord took away David's sins, and just like the example with Moses, David offered no sacrifice at all except maybe a broken and contrite heart. The Lord's forgiveness has never been conditioned upon a sacrifice of atonement!

For years and consistent with most Christian theology, I was taught and believed that Jesus's shed blood was the basis by which God forgave our sins. However, I was always confused by 1 Corinthians 15:17, which states that if Christ had not been raised, we would still be in our sins. My belief system for forgiveness of sins was mistakenly tied to the shedding of Christ's blood, not to His resurrection. Therefore, I often struggled with 1 Corinthians 15:17, and recognized that it did not fit with the concept that only "the shedding of blood was necessary for forgiveness and remission of sin." The verse was incongruent with how I understood forgiveness. To state the same point differently, the traditional belief system with regard to forgiveness of sins was tied to the shedding of blood, but not to the resurrection. The resurrection was great and wonderful—sort of like icing on the cake—but since Jesus shed His blood, I could never understand how I would still be in my sins even if Christ had not been raised. Because Jesus shed His blood, even if He were not raised, at least our sins still should have been forgiven under my prior mistaken understanding of the Gospel. If the sacrifice and shedding of blood were necessary to forgive sins, then it did not make sense that we were still in our sins if Christ had not been resurrected. I never quite knew what to make of 1 Corinthians 15:17, but I now have a path that makes it congruent with the Gospel.

Based upon the above, I have now come to realize that if Christ were not raised, we would still *be under the power of sin,* even though *our sins would be forgiven.* Therefore, if 1 Corinthians 15:3 and 17 were referring to "sin" rather than "sins," such an interpretation would be consistent with everything I have shared. Because if Christ had not been raised—if He did not defeat death by and through His resurrection—we would still be subject to the consequences of sin, which is death. If Christ had not been raised, we would still be and always will be subject to the power of sin (without ever the possibility of overcoming sin), which is empowered by death. Therefore, the victory of Christ's resurrection is the victory over death and the power of sin,[2] rather than his resurrection being necessary for the forgiveness of sins. As a result, I am convinced that the words "sin" in 1 Corinthians 15:3 and 17 are actually referring to the power of sin. Romans 6:7 gives further support to the conclusion: "because anyone who has died has been set free from sin." (Also, see Romans 6:18, 22.) The writer of Hebrews explains that Jesus's death outside the camp was for the purpose of sanctifying us; Jesus's death was not in order that our sins could be forgiven. "Therefore Jesus also suffered outside the gate, that He might sanctify the people through His own blood" (Hebrews 13:12).

But what about Hebrews 9:22: "In fact, the law requires that nearly everything be cleansed with blood, and without the shedding of blood there is no forgiveness." In the first instance, this verse is addressed to "everything" rather than "everyone." From the law, we know that utensils and articles in the temple were cleansed or made holy by sprinkling with blood. When you look at the Greek word translated as "forgiveness," Strong's first definition is "release

---

2. Hebrews 9:26: "Otherwise, He would have needed to suffer often since the foundation of the world; but now once at the consummation of the ages He has been *revealed to put away sin* by the sacrifice of Himself."

from bondage or imprisonment," meaning that the verse may be more accurately translated if it read, "In fact, the law requires that nearly everything be cleansed with blood, and without the shedding of blood there is no release from bondage or imprisonment." Further, this verse is explaining the law rather than the Gospel or the cross.

With regard to the latter part of the verse concerning forgiveness, the Gospel is not an exact replica of the law; the law is only a shadow of the good things to come. A shadow is a vague outline of a figure. A shadow provides no details, and it can greatly exaggerate the size of the figure or greatly minimize the size of the figure. If you look at a shadow of me, it would be a totally inadequate tool for you to use to describe me. You would not know any of the details about me. The best you could do is compare my shadow to another person's shadow to determine who is taller or bigger, but you would not be able to determine my age, height, hair color, profession, or status. You would not be able to determine my disposition.

In this instance, the shadow is pointing to "forgiveness," but in the New Covenant, forgiveness comes from the decision of God, not by providing a blood sacrifice. The shadow is also pointing to the amazing victory over the power of sin. John 1: 14 "And the Word became flesh, and dwelt among us; and we saw His glory, glory as of the only Son from the Father, full of grace and truth." And John 1:17 "For the Law was given through Moses; grace and truth [came to be] realized through Jesus Christ." Grace is always more generous, more complete, and more unconditional than a provision coming through the law. To rely upon the law, which is only a vague shadow "of the good things to come and not the form of those things itself,"[3] to define the form, the specifics, and the details of New Testament forgiveness, would restrict us to living and receiving under law rather than living under grace. The law should never define the scope or the specifics of grace; its purpose is only to foreshadow it.

---

3. Hebrews 10:1

Galatians 1:4 "who gave Himself for our sins so that He might rescue us from this present evil age, according to the will of our God and Father," may be another verse that, on initial readings, seems to be incongruent with the above and suggests penal substitution. Rather than repeating the discussion above, I will simply point out that Galatians 1:4 does not espouse sacrifice in order to obtain forgiveness of sins. Still, the primary focus of the verse is to explain that the Messiah sacrificed Himself in order that He would rescue us from the power of sin. This concept is entirely consistent with the truth that Jesus, through His death and resurrection, broke the power of sin and death. And Messiah sacrificed Himself "so that through death He might destroy the one who has the power of death, that is, the devil" (Hebrews 2:14), and in so doing, to completely and totally destroy the power of death.

We cannot leave this topic without addressing Revelation 13:8 "the Lamb who was slain from the creation of the world." Jesus was indeed the Lamb slain from before time. The question is not whether Jesus was slain but whether Jesus was slain in substitution of the death that we deserved. Stated differently, did God require Jesus's substitutionary death in order to forgive our sins? The above discussion is exceedingly persuasive that God freely chooses to forgive humanity's collective sins, but does that contradict Revelation 13:8? A principle of interpretation that I learned years ago was that the first mention of a concept is particularly important to understanding the concept.

The first mention of a lamb or a ram is in Genesis 15:8–18, an account of when the Lord appeared to Abraham and promised him numerous descendants. Abraham questioned how he will possess the promise, and the Lord responded in verse 9 "Bring Me a three-year-old heifer, a three-year-old female goat, a three-year-old ram, a turtledove, and a young pigeon." After Abraham bought Him the animals, the Lord cut them in two, laid each half opposite, and on that day "made a covenant with Abraham." The sacrifice of the ram or lamb was not a sin offering and it was not to atone for sins, *but to initiate the covenant promise.* With the sacrifice of the ram, the Lord guaranteed that He would fulfill His promise. It was the guarantee that His word would be fulfilled; it was the guarantee that He would fulfill His word. Jesus, the lamb slain from the foundations of the world, was not to pay the price for sins, but to fulfill the better covenant. "By the same extent Jesus also has become the guarantee of a better covenant" (Hebrews 7:22).

Let's also look at Genesis 22, which is Abraham's offering of Isaac. This story is often compared to the New Covenant sacrifice of Jesus on the cross. We have assumed that it was an offering to atone for sins. But looking more closely, we will see that it was not a sin offering at all.

> Isaac spoke to his father Abraham and said, "My father.'" And he said, "Here I am, my son." And he said, "Look, the fire and the wood, but where is the lamb for the burnt offering?" [8]Abraham said, "God will provide for Himself the lamb for the burnt offering, my son." So the two of them walked on together. [9]Then they came to the place of which God had told him; and Abraham built the altar there and arranged the wood, and bound his son Isaac and laid him on the altar, on top of the wood. [10]And Abraham reached out with his hand and took the knife to slaughter his son. [11]But the angel of the LORD called to him from heaven and said, "Abraham, Abraham!" And he said, "Here I am." [12]He said, "Do not reach out your hand against the boy, and do not do anything to him; for now I know that you fear God, since you have not withheld your son, your only son, from Me" (Genesis 22:7-12).

This, however, is not the end of the story. "Then Abraham raised his eyes and looked, and behold, behind him was a *ram* caught in the thicket by its horns; and Abraham went and took the *ram* and offered it up as a *burnt offering* in the place of his son" (Genesis 22:13). Notice that God did not require the ram offering in order to spare Isaac. Isaac was spared because of the word of the Lord, and then Abraham offered a burnt offering. Both verse 7 and verse 13 explicitly tell us that Abraham was offering a burnt offering. He was not offering a sin offering.

What was the purpose of a burnt offering? After Genesis 22, the next reference to a burnt offering is recorded in Exodus 18 when

Moses's father-in-law meets him and "Moses told his father-in-law everything that the LORD had done to Pharaoh and the Egyptians for Israel's sake, all the hardship that had confronted them on the journey, and how the LORD had rescued them" (verse 8). After hearing all the goodness which the LORD had done for Israel in rescuing them from the hand of the Egyptians, Jethro rejoiced (verse 9). "Then Jethro, Moses's father-in-law, took a burnt offering and sacrifices for God, and Aaron came with all the elders of Israel to eat a meal with Moses's father-in-law before God" (Exodus 18:12). Again, we see that the burnt offering was not a sin offering and it was not to atone for any sins. It was a celebration of what the LORD had done in bringing the Israelites out of slavery in Egypt.

Looking at Exodus 29 provides a description of the sin offering and the burnt offering. The sin offering, described in verses 10–14, required the slaughter of a bull, rather than a lamb. By contrast, the burnt offering, described in verses 15–18, required the slaughter of a ram or lamb. When the writer of Hebrews stated that the sacrificial system was incapable of removing sin, the writer states, "the blood of bulls and goats can't take away sins."[4] Why didn't the writer say that the blood of rams or lambs can't take away sin; because bulls and goats, rather than lambs, were offered as a sin offering in the Old Covenant sacrificial system? Jesus was never, ever, referred to as a bull or a goat. Jesus was the lamb, the burnt offering, slain from the foundations of the world, as a guarantee of the better covenant.

Once again, in Hebrews, we see that Jesus's death and resurrection were for the purpose of establishing the new eternal covenant of Life. "Now may the God of peace, who brought up from the dead the great Shepherd of the sheep through the blood of the eternal covenant, that is, Jesus our Lord" (Hebrews 13:20). Jesus was not crucified as a sin offering, because Love does not require an offering or a sacrifice in order to forgive. Love forgives because Love forgives. But Love will also sacrifice itself for your freedom and your life. Jesus's death was a demonstration of Love. Jesus's death was the evidence and the expression of God's Love, rather

4. Hebrews 10:4

than an expression of God's wrath or anger. Paul says it well in Romans 5:7-8: "Very rarely will anyone die for a righteous person, though for a good person someone might possibly dare to die. ⁸But God *demonstrates his own love* for us in this: While we were still sinners, Christ died for us." God demonstrates his love for us through the cross, and at the same time, Jesus's death establishes the new eternal covenant of Life. Jesus, the lamb slain from the foundations of the world, set us free from slavery to sin by breaking the power of sin, and it fits perfectly with the fact that God also caused us to be born again.

# Chapter 11

## God Caused Us to be Born Again

Now I am really going to challenge ingrained thinking. In our evangelical world, everything has revolved around "being born again." Yet Jesus mentioned being born again only in one discourse with Nicodemus, using a metaphor which has taken a life of its own. We find Jesus's conversation in John 3:3: "Jesus responded and said to him, 'Truly, truly, I say to you, unless someone is born again, he cannot see the kingdom of God.'" And again in John 3:5: "Jesus answered, 'Truly, truly, I say to you, unless someone is born of water and the Spirit, he cannot enter the kingdom of God.'" The first important comment is that Jesus's discourse with Nicodemus is about the Kingdom of God, not about justification or what we commonly refer to as salvation. It is about receiving abundant life. Remember the Kingdom of God is the rule and reign of God in every aspect, and it is much, much more than justification. Jesus is saying if you are going to live in My Kingdom, which functions differently from all the other kingdoms of man and this world, you will have to have such a different perspective that your old man will have to die, and you will have to live as an entirely new man.

Being good religious people who gravitate toward rules and certainty, rather than receiving the gift of having been born again by Jesus's work, we developed a process (or many different processes) so that people can be born again according to our theology. But Jesus's only discourse on being born again does not prescribe a process. Christianity has created a process to get where we rightfully thought we were supposed to be, without realizing that God had already accomplished that work by placing us in Christ. And I remind you that as I reviewed Acts to see what the apostles taught, they proclaimed forgiveness of sins but never proclaimed a process in which to adhere. Being born again is never referred to in Acts when the Greek and Roman world was being evangelized. In every new city in Europe that Paul and the apostles evangelized, there was not one mention of being born again. Was that oversight, or did Paul have a different, more complete understanding of the Gospel?

Expanding on John 3:5, we are born of water when we are born naturally. When are we born of the Spirit? I grew up being taught this occurred when we "asked Jesus into our heart" or when we "repented and recited the sinner's prayer." But according to 1 Peter 1:3, we are born of the Spirit when we are resurrected with Christ after having been buried with Him. So you may see what I am contemplating: that we were born again long before we ever recited the sinner's prayer or even before we were born naturally. Before the foundations of the world, God caused you to be born again. Are you seeing that this is actually Good News beyond our wildest comprehension? The problem is that this Good News shatters the processes in which we have trusted.

Who decided whether you are born of water? Not you, not the person being born, your parents or ultimately God decided. The one being born plays no part in the decision to be born. Who decides if we are born of the Spirit? According to John 1:13, we are born not by the will of man, but by God: "who were born, not of blood, nor of the will of the flesh, nor of the will of a man, but of God." Based upon 1 Peter 1:3, it is not the person being reborn, but God who causes us to be reborn or born again. 1 Peter 1:3:

"Blessed be the God and Father of our Lord Jesus Christ, who according to His great mercy has caused us to be born again to a living hope through the resurrection of Jesus Christ from the dead." Notice the tense of the verb. God caused us to be born again. You did not cause yourself to be born again. God did! According to 1 Peter 1:3, in being born again, we are passive; we do nothing; we are acted upon. So, how are we born again? By Christ's death and resurrection and because of being in Christ when He was crucified and resurrected, we are born again into the new Christ lineage. It is simply God's plan for the full and complete redemption of mankind. Romans 6:4–8 is the description of being born again.

> Therefore, we have been buried with Him through baptism into death, so that as Christ was raised from the dead through the glory of the Father, so we too might walk in newness of life. $^5$For if we have become united with Him in the likeness of His death, certainly we shall also be His resurrection, $^6$knowing this, that our old man was crucified with Him, in order that our body of sin might be done away with, so that we would no longer be slaves to sin.

This all occurs because God placed us in Christ before the foundations of the world, as is clearly described in 2 Corinthians 1:21 and Ephesians 1:3–4. As we conclude the topic of *What God Has Done for Us*—a portion of which includes placing us in Christ, breaking the power of sin and death, and causing us to be born again—we see that these three aspects are not actually separate and distinctive works at all. These beautiful works are as interdependent as the Trinity. One cannot exist without the other, but I thought they would be better understood as a complete work if I addressed them individually to the best of my understanding.

# Chapter 12

## What is the Gospel?

I HAVE TAKEN 11 chapters endeavoring to describe the Good News of the Gospel. Does that mean that the Gospel is too complex to be understood by the average person if it takes 11 chapters to describe it? Does it mean that you have to understand Greek to understand the Gospel? Of course, the answer is "No." Truthfully, it would have taken just a few words if we did not have to unlearn so much of what we have been taught incorrectly. I played basketball through high school and then recreationally for several more years. Basketball came pretty naturally to me. I also coached Upward Basketball for 10 years. One of my biggest concerns with first graders playing basketball is that, with their small size and limited strength, they never learned how to hold and shoot the basketball correctly. They heaved the ball. They never used the correct form for a layup. It was more like a "sling up." That means they learned incorrectly, and later in life, it would take more time to unlearn the improper form before they could start shooting with the right form. It is similar to anything, and especially with the Gospel. The Gospel is simple and profound, but our religious training has created impediments to hearing and understanding.

John 3:16 would go a long way in accurately conveying the message of the Gospel if we really believed it and interpreted it in accordance with the principles set out above, and if we combined it with John 3:17 so that it would be less likely to be taken out of context. However, our more common actual interpretation of the verse is likely "For God was so angry at the world, that He caused His only Son to suffer and die, so that He could have a legal reason to forgive some of the world and so that some of the world will spend eternity in heaven rather than in hell, but of course, the rest of the world will spend eternity in hell."

How unfortunate and inaccurate that most of us were taught that "the world" did not include all of humanity; that there were people who God did not love and people that God did not rescue. Even Strong's concordance defines the world as the "inhabitants of the earth, men, the human family" and "the ungodly multitude; the whole mass of men alienated from God, and therefore hostile to the cause of Christ." In addition, John 3:16 does not differentiate between heaven and hell, but rather between life and death. God has always been inviting us to receive His abundant life, but too often "life" is only marketed as an alternative to and an escape from eternal hell, rather than being the highest form of living. Somehow, we concluded that avoiding hell was the Good News. How could we have concluded that avoiding hell was the extent of the "Good News?"

What is the Gospel, then? The Gospel is that we are in Christ and have been in Christ since the foundation of the world—that by being in Christ, our old man (old Adamic nature) was crucified with Christ and that we were resurrected with Christ as a new man. We have moved from death to life; from Adam's bloodline to Jesus's bloodline; from darkness to light; from slavery to sin to freedom in Christ. The Gospel is that you are and that you have always been God's beloved, dear, precious, adored, accepted son or daughter. That is the meaning of Romans 8:19: "For the eagerly awaiting creation waits for the revealing of the sons and daughters of God." Strong's defines "revealing" as "a disclosure of truth, instruction, concerning divine things before unknown." We have always been beloved sons and daughters of God, and we will always be beloved sons and daughters of God, but we have not always known that we were always dearly beloved sons and daughters of God. However, this truth of our identify is being faithfully and graciously revealed.

The Gospel is that God has accomplished everything for us that needs to be done. As we come to trust God, we learn to become receivers of what has always been true. Lastly, since you are predestined to be God's beloved, dear, precious, adored, accepted son or daughter, nothing can change that. The enemy cannot steal your status and position with God. The enemy's only weapon is to try to convince you that you are not who God declares you to be. If he does, you will live below the standard of who you really are. You are a beloved and accepted child of the King, have always been, and will always be, but you can live as the child of slaves until you come to know who you are. In summary, the Gospel is simply that you are God's child, that you have always been, and that you will always be His beloved and accepted child. Good News indeed.

## THE GOSPEL IS ALWAYS AN INVITATION

At the beginning of the book, I asked the question, "What has God done for us?" In response, I summarized that God did everything for us before expounding upon the specifics of His work. Because God has done everything necessary for the fulfillment of the Gospel, I have begun to realize that everything from God is an invitation, never a requirement; that everything from God is an invitation rather than an obligation. Because God has done everything necessary for the fulfillment of the Gospel, we don't need to earn the abundant life that the Gospel makes possible. Rather than earning, we only receive what His work has already accomplished and is accomplishing. Bad religion has re-characterized God's invitations in the Gospel as obligatory. Therefore, God's very sincere love-motivated invitations are too often perceived as obligations backed by threats of punishment.

Why do I assert that "bad religion" has re-characterized God's invitations as obligations? Isn't it good to "incentivize" people to follow God, to serve, and to participate in community? Invitations create excitement and joy; the message from being invited is that you are included, welcome, and wanted. The message of obligation is that your work and your effort are more important than who you are. And worst of all, obligations steal our joy from engagement and participation. Bad religion takes the joy from following Christ and seeking His plans, and makes following Christ obligatory and a burden backed up with threats of hell, judgment, and separation. Then bad religion tries to market that obligation and burden to others as Good News.

In my own life, I am hearing only invitations from God. The Gospel should no longer create obligatory responses, but *emphatic invitations* for more abundant life. As a result, every aspect of the Gospel should be viewed as God's invitation for you to experience a more abundant life. When Paul writes to Philemon, he states that he could order Philemon "to do what is proper, yet for love's sake I rather appeal to you" (Philemon 8–9). One of the definitions of "appeal" is to invite or exhort. Paul clearly expresses that because of the value of relationships, he prioritizes love over obligation, just as God invites in love rather than commanding or obligating in power. Once again, doing so is the nature of Love.

Although God is faithfully communicating to our hearts, I have never heard the audible voice of God. Because I hear His voice in my heart or spirit, I interpret His emphasis, and I *perceive or assume His tone* according to my expectations of how He acts. If I expect God to be harsh or angry, I perceive His words to me as coming from a harsh or angry demeanor, even though it is not true. If I expect God to be loving and compassionate, I perceive His words as a salve that heals. That means that although God is always speaking gentle and loving words, I may interpret them as harsh words coming from an angry God and especially if His invitation follows my failure. One of God's consistent and repetitive invitations is "Come to Me." In recent years, I have realized that God is always inviting us to "Come to Him." When I fail, God invites me to come sit on His lap. When I follow or obey, God invites me to come to Him. When I feel lonely, God invites me to come to Him.

But I did not always hear God's words "Come to Me" as an invitation. Because my view of God was incorrect, because I thought He was harsh and angry, I inferred a tone in His words that misrepresented His heart. It is easy to understand that a parent's words "Come to Me" can create excitement or anxiety depending on the tone. The child's response depends upon the tone of the parent's voice. The tone of God's voice is always gentle, kind, compassionate, and loving, but if we have a wrong view of God's heart, we will more likely perceive a harsh tone. The same is true with God's invitations under the Gospel. God is always inviting us to abundant life, but if we misperceive His heart and His tone, we will see His invitations as obligations backed by threats of punishment. Threats of punishment never build relationships of trust. Obligations never build relationships of trust. Because God wants us to trust Him and enter into a loving relationship, He is continually inviting us to participate with Him in abundant life.

## THE CHURCH'S FUNCTION

We have identified a relationship with God that is based upon receiving rather than earning; that is based upon being rather than doing; that is based upon recognizing what is already true about you rather than efforts at self-improvement. If the preceding chapters are substantially correct, that means we do not have to craft the correct prayer of forgiveness in order to be forgiven, that we do not need to be baptized in order to come into God's family, and that we do not need to participate in communion or mass in order to stay in good standing with God. But that also means that some of you are fearful that this description of the Gospel guts the need for the local church, which is very dear to you.

Some of you are fearful that the workers in the Kingdom will stop working for the Kingdom. Given that concern, what is the role of the local church in empowering humanity to live the Good News? From my perspective, the local church's greatest opportunity is to introduce and present God who is our life, accurately, and to remind men and women of their intrinsic value and worth because they have been created in the likeness and image of God; to remind men and women how God views them and what God says about them. The Lord has invited the local church to help men and women identify and recognize lies that each of us believes about God and about ourselves. The local church should be a loud voice of truth in the face of Satan's lies.

Paul emphasizes the church's function in Ephesians 3:10: "His intent was that now, through the church, the manifold wisdom of God should be made known to the rulers and authorities in the heavenly realms." Some principalities and powers function in this world by deceiving the minds of individuals. If the principalities and powers can persuade you to believe a lie about God, about yourself, or about someone else, it will take away some degree of your abundant life. The church is commissioned to speak the truth into a world filled with lies about God, lies about our value and worth, and lies about the value and worth of other individuals. And it takes a corporate function to uncover and realize lies and misrepresentations about God.

I have endeavored to do my part in uncovering misrepresentations. I have been influenced throughout my life by people who had a greater understanding than I did. For teachers and writers, it was people who are unknown in most church circles—Fuchsia Pickett, Alan Vincent, Francis Frangipane, Steve Sampson, Wayne Jacobsen, and Watchman Nee. Followers of Christ who had compelling messages and rich fruit, like John Lynch, Jamie Winship, Paul Young, and Brad Jersak, gave me permission to think outside the box. Christ Fellowship even had a sermon series entitled "Outside the Box." In the last 5 years, it has included more personal connections within our local congregation in Kingsport, Tennessee, especially when Jamie and Donna Winship moved to Kingsport in 2022. All of these worked together just as God designed, and all triggered questions or influenced focus. Some listened well. I have had a sounding board to ask questions and share what I thought God was revealing, especially with my wife, Diane. I gave people whom I trusted the right to tell me if I was off base. I relied not only on the Spirit of Truth directly, but people who walked by and listened to the Spirit of Truth. I began to recognize that when people responded out of fear, including myself, and I realized that responses based on fear were not reflecting God's heart.

I have prayed for our area with a small group of friends for 25 years. Often, I would run concepts by them to see if I was missing the mark. I learned from 1 Corinthians 14:26 that isolation or independence would not be useful to understanding God's heart, and in places of safe and loving community, God blessed my contemplations and study. In the community, I learned how to listen and ask God questions, and I moved away from trying to convince God to move in someone's life because I have learned that I could trust the most kind, good, and loving Person ever, knowing that His only desire is to bless us with abundant life.

I began to realize who I had always been by God's decree, and little by little gave up trying to gain men's approval. I realized that the truest thing about me is what God says, not what I think or perceive, and certainly not what others think. I began to believe that I cannot become who I already am, but that I can begin to believe and live what is already true and what has always been true about me. And you can too! Ask the Lord what He wants you to know about yourself. Ask Him to show you who you are in the deepest core. You will be pleasantly surprised. In your deepest core, flow rivers of living water. In your deepest core is life-giving substance. In your deepest core, you are pure and holy, created in the image of God. But if you do not believe these truths about your inner person, you will try to create externally what you perceive as lacking in your inner person. And you will return to earning and striving rather than receiving.

Also, ask Him to reveal to you any aspect of the Good News that has eluded you. Lastly, I challenge you to stand and speak in the temple, in the church, in the market, in your home, in the neighborhood, in the education system, and tell the people all the words of this incredible, abundant life. Be like Paul, who in his farewell to the Ephesians declared, "I did not shrink from declaring to you the whole purpose of God" (Acts 20:27). The Gospel is called Good News for a reason! Believe the Good News; receive the Good News; share the Good News; and declare the Good News!

# Appendix A

## *Passages from Acts that record what the apostles declared or preached.*

Acts 2:11 Cretans and Arabs—we hear them speaking in our own tongues of the mighty deeds of God.

Acts 4:2 being greatly disturbed because they were teaching the people and proclaiming in Jesus the resurrection from the dead.

Acts 4:20 for we cannot stop speaking about what we have seen and heard.

Acts 4:33 And with great power the apostles were giving testimony to the resurrection of the Lord Jesus, and abundant grace was upon them all.

Acts 5:20 "Go, stand and speak to the people in the temple area the whole message of this Life."

Acts 8:12 But when they believed Philip as he was preaching the good news about the kingdom of God and the name of Jesus Christ, both men and women were being baptized

Acts 8:35 Then Philip opened his mouth, and beginning from this Scripture he preached Jesus to him.

Acts 9:20 and immediately he began to proclaim Jesus in the synagogues, saying, "He is the Son of God."

## APPENDIX A

Acts 11:20 But there were some of them, men of Cyprus and Cyrene, who came to Antioch and began speaking to the Greeks as well, preaching the good news of the Lord Jesus.

Acts 13:5 When they reached Salamis, they began to proclaim the word of God in the synagogues of the Jews; and they also had John as their helper.

Acts 13:32 "And we preach to you the good news of the promise made to the fathers,"

Acts 13:38–39 "Therefore let it be known to you, brothers, that through Him forgiveness of sins is proclaimed to you, 39and through Him everyone who believes is freed from all things, from which you could not be freed through the Law of Moses."

Acts 14:7 and there they continued to preach the Gospel

Acts 14:21 And after they had preached the Gospel to that city and had made a good number of disciples, they returned to Lystra, to Iconium, and to Antioch

Acts 16:31–32 They said, "Believe in the Lord Jesus, and you will be saved, you and your household." 32And they spoke the word of God to him together with all who were in his house.

Acts 17:30 So having overlooked the times of ignorance, God is now proclaiming to mankind that all people everywhere are to repent,

Acts 18: 5 But when Silas and Timothy came down from Macedonia, Paul began devoting himself completely to the word, testifying to the Jews that Jesus was the Christ.

Acts 19:8 And he entered the synagogue and continued speaking out boldly for three months, having discussions and persuading them about the kingdom of God.

Acts 20: 21 solemnly testifying to both Jews and Greeks of repentance toward God and faith in our Lord Jesus Christ.

Acts 20:24 But I[Paul] do not consider my life of any account as dear to myself, so that I may finish my course and the

## APPENDIX A

ministry which I received from the Lord Jesus, to testify solemnly of the Gospel of God's grace.

Acts 26:18 to open their eyes so that they may turn from darkness to light, and from the power of Satan to God, that they may receive forgiveness of sins and an inheritance among those who have been sanctified by faith in Me.' "Receive" forgiveness indicates that it is already there, but it needs to be believed and accepted. It is not to "receive the Lord Jesus Christ," but to receive forgiveness.

Acts 28:23 When they had set a day for Paul, they came to him at his lodging in large numbers; and he was explaining to them by solemnly testifying about the kingdom of God and trying to persuade them concerning Jesus, from both the Law of Moses and from the Prophets, from morning until evening.

Acts 28:30–31 And he stayed two full years in his own rented quarters and was welcoming all who came to him, [31]preaching the kingdom of God and teaching concerning the Lord Jesus Christ with all openness, unhindered.

# Appendix B
## "ALL" Verses

The Greek Word 3956 means "each, every, any, all, the whole, everyone, all things, everything."

The Greek Word 3745 mans "as great as, as far as, how much, how many, whoever."

Genesis 1:31 And God saw all that He had made, and behold, it was very good. And there was evening and there was morning, the sixth day.

Genesis 12:3 And I will bless those who bless you, And the one who curses you I will curse. And in you all the families of the earth will be blessed.

Genesis 18:18 since Abraham will certainly become a great and mighty nation, and in him all the nations of the earth will be blessed?

Genesis 22:18 "And in your seed all the nations of the earth shall be blessed, because you have obeyed My voice."

Psalm 106:48 Blessed be the LORD, the God of Israel, From everlasting to everlasting. And all the people shall say, "Amen." Praise the LORD!

Isaiah 25:8 He will swallow up death for all time, And the Lord GOD will wipe tears away from all faces, And He will remove

## APPENDIX B

the disgrace of His people from all the earth; For the LORD has spoken.

Jeremiah 31:34 "They will not teach again, each one his neighbor and each one his brother, saying, 'Know the LORD,' for they will all know Me, from the least of them to the greatest of them," declares the LORD, "for I will forgive their wrongdoing, and their sin I will no longer remember."

Mark 3:28–29 "Truly I say to you, all [3956] sins will be forgiven the sons and daughters of men, and whatever blasphemies they commit; $^{29}$but whoever blasphemes against the Holy Spirit never has forgiveness, but is guilty of an eternal sin"—(Also, Luke 12:10)

Luke 3:6 "AND ALL [3956] FLESH WILL SEE THE SALVATION OF GOD!'"

Luke 20:38 "Now He is not the God of the dead, but of the living; for all [3956] live to Him."

John 1:7 He came as a witness, to testify about the Light, so that all [3956] might believe through him.

John 1:9 This was the true Light that, coming into the world, enlightens every [3956] person.

John 1:16 For of His fullness we have all [3956] received, and grace upon grace.

John 6:45 "It is written in the Prophets: 'AND THEY SHALL ALL [3956] BE TAUGHT OF GOD.' Everyone who has heard and learned from the Father, comes to Me."

John 12:32 "And I, if I am lifted up from the earth, will draw all [3956] people to Myself."

Acts 17:30 So having overlooked the times of ignorance, God is now proclaiming to mankind that all [3956] people everywhere are to repent,

Romans 2:12 For all [3745] who have sinned without the Law will also perish without the Law, and all [3745] who have sinned under the Law will be judged by the Law;

## APPENDIX B

Romans 3:22–24 even the righteousness of God through faith in Jesus Christ for all those who believe; for there is no distinction; [23]for all [3956] have sinned and fall short of the glory of God, [24]being justified as a gift by His grace through the redemption which is in Christ Jesus;

Romans 4:16 For this reason it is by faith, in order that it may be in accordance with grace, so that the promise will be guaranteed to all [3956] the descendants, not only to those who are of the Law, but also to those who are of the faith of Abraham, who is the father of us all [3956],

Romans 5:12 Therefore, just as through one man sin entered into the world, and death through sin, and so death spread to all [3956] mankind, because all [3956] sinned—

Romans 5:18 So then, as through one offense the result was condemnation to all [3956] mankind, so also through one act of righteousness the result was justification of life to all [3956] mankind.

Romans 8:32 He who did not spare His own Son, but delivered Him over for us all [3956], how will He not also with Him freely give us all [3956] things?

Romans 11:26 and so all [3956] Israel will be saved; just as it is written: "THE DELIVERER WILL COME FROM ZION, HE WILL REMOVE UNGODLINESS FROM JACOB."

Romans 11:32 For God has shut up all [3956] in disobedience, so that He may show mercy to all [3956].

1 Corinthians 12:6 [Speaking about the various gifts] There are varieties of effects, but the same God who works all [3956] things in all [3956] persons.

1 Corinthians 12:13 For by one Spirit we were all [3956] baptized into one body, whether Jews or Greeks, whether slaves or free, and we were all [3956] made to drink of one Spirit.

1 Corinthians 15:22 For as in Adam all [3956] die, so also in Christ all [3956] will be made alive.

## APPENDIX B

1 Corinthians 15:51 Behold, I am telling you a mystery; we will not all [3956] sleep, but we will all [3956] be changed

2 Corinthians 3:18 But we all [3956], with unveiled faces, looking as in a mirror at the glory of the Lord, are being transformed into the same image from glory to glory, just as from the Lord, the Spirit.

2 Corinthians 5:14 For the love of Christ controls us, having concluded this, that one died for all [3956], therefore all [3956] died;

2 Corinthians 5:15 and He died for all [3956], so that those who live would no longer live for themselves, but for Him who died and rose on their behalf.

Galatians 3:26 For you are all [3956] sons and daughters of God through faith in Christ Jesus.

Galatians 3:27 For all of you [3745] who were baptized into Christ have clothed yourselves with Christ.

Galatians 3:28 There is neither Jew nor Greek, there is neither slave nor free, there is neither male nor female; for you are all [3956] one in Christ Jesus.

Ephesians 4:6 one God and Father of all [3956] who is over all [3956] and through all [3956] and in all [3956].

Ephesians 4:13 until we all [3956] attain to the unity of the faith, and of the knowledge of the Son of God, to a mature man, to the measure of the stature which belongs to the fullness of Christ.

Colossians 1:20 and through Him to reconcile all things to Himself, whether things on earth or things in heaven, having made peace through the blood of His cross.

Colossians 1:28 We proclaim Him, admonishing every [3956] person and teaching every [3956] person with all [3956] wisdom, so that we may present every [3956] person complete in Christ.

## APPENDIX B

Colossians 2:13 And when you were dead in your wrongdoings and the uncircumcision of your flesh, He made you alive together with Him, having forgiven us all [3956] our wrongdoings.

Colossians 3:11 a renewal in which there is no distinction between Greek and Jew, circumcised and uncircumcised, barbarian, Scythian, slave, and free, but Christ is all [3956], and in all [3956].

I Thessalonians 5:5 for you are all [3956] sons of light and sons of day. We are not of night nor of darkness;

2 Thessalonians 2:12 in order that they all [3956] may be judged who did not believe the truth, but took pleasure in wickedness.

2 Thessalonians 3:2 and that we will be rescued from troublesome and evil people; for not all [3956] have the faith.

1 Timothy 2:4 who wants all [3956] people to be saved and to come to the knowledge of the truth.

1 Timothy 2:6 who gave Himself as a ransom for all [3956], the testimony given at the proper time.

1 Timothy 4:10 For it is for this we labor and strive, because we have set our hope on the living God, who is the Savior of all [3956] mankind, especially of believers.

Titus 2:11 For the grace of God has appeared, bringing salvation to all [3956] people,

Hebrews 2:9 But we do see Him who was made for a little while lower than the angels, namely, Jesus, because of His suffering death crowned with glory and honor, so that by the grace of God He might taste death [experience] for everyone [3956].

Hebrews 5:9 And having been perfected, He became the source of eternal salvation for all [3956] those who obey Him,

Hebrews 7:27 who does not need daily, like those high priests, to offer up sacrifices, first for His own sins and then for the

## APPENDIX B

sins of the people, because this He did once for all when He offered up Himself.

Hebrews 8:11 "AND THEY WILL NOT TEACH, EACH ONE HIS FELLOW CITIZEN, AND EACH ONE HIS BROTHER, SAYING, 'KNOW THE LORD,' FOR THEY WILL ALL [3956] KNOW ME, FROM THE LEAST TO THE GREATEST OF THEM."

James 1:5 But if any of you lacks wisdom, let him ask of God, who gives to all [3956] generously and without reproach, and it will be given to him.

1 Peter 3:18 For Christ also suffered for sins once for all [530] time, the just for the unjust, so that He might bring us to God, having been put to death in the flesh, but made alive in the spirit;

2 Peter 3:9 The Lord is not slow about His promise, as some count slowness, but is patient toward you, not willing for any to perish, but for all [3956] to come to repentance.

I John 2:2 and He Himself is the propitiation for our sins; and not for ours only, but also for the sins of the whole [3650—all, whole, and completely] world.

# Bibliography

Frangipane, Francis. In Christ Image Level I training email dated December 13, 2002.

Frangipane, Francis. *The Place of Immunity*. Cedar Rapids, IA: Arrow Publications, 1994.

Lloyd-Jones, Martyn. *Romans: An Exposition of Chapter 6, The New Man*. London: Banner of Truth Trust, 1972.

MacDonald, Gregory. *The Evangelical Universalist*. Eugene, OR: Cascade, 2012.

Rillera, Andrew Remington. *Lamb of the Free*. Eugene, OR: Cascade, 2024.

Willard, Dallas. *The Great Omission: Reclaiming Jesus's Essential Teachings on Discipleship*. San Francisco: HarperOne, 2006.

# Index of Scriptures Referenced in Chapter 6

| | | | |
|---|---|---|---|
| Numbers 14:19–20 | 56 | Romans 10:10 | 62 |
| Matthew 9:2 | 56 | 2 Corinthians 5:19 | 52–54 |
| Matthew 18:21–35 | 64–65 | Galatians 2:16 | 60 |
| Mark 2:5 | 56 | Galatians 2:20 | 61 |
| | | Galatians 3:2 | 61 |
| Luke 5:20 | 56 | Galatians 3:5 | 61 |
| Luke 7:36–50 | 56 | Galatians 4:1 | 60 |
| Luke 23:34 | 57 | | |
| Luke 24:45–47 | 55 | Ephesians 1:7 | 63 |
| | | Ephesians 2:8 | 58 |
| Acts 4:20 | 54 | | |
| Acts 13:38 | 53 | Colossians 2:13 | 53 |
| Acts 13:38–39 | 54 | Colossians 3:13 | 53, 64 |
| Acts 26:16–18 | 55 | | |
| | | Philippians 3:9 | 61–62 |
| Romans 3:22 | 61 | | |
| Romans 4:3 | 59 | Hebrews 8:12 | 58 |
| Romans 4:5 | 59 | | |
| Romans 5:1 | 62–63 | Titus 3:5 | 68 |
| Romans 6:1–2 | 67 | | |
| Romans 6:23 | 66 | 1 John 3:15 | 66 |